Just The facts101

Textbook Key Facts

Microsoft Publisher 2013

Comprehensive

by Cram101

Textbook NOT Included

Table of Contents

Just The Facts101

Exam Prep for

Microsoft Publisher 2013
Comprehensive

Just The Facts101 Exam Prep is your link from
the textbook and lecture to your exams.

**Just The Facts101 Exam Preps are unauthorized and comprehensive reviews
of your textbooks.**

All material provided by CTI Publications (c) 2019

Textbook publishers and textbook authors do not participate in or contribute to these reviews.

Just The Facts101 Exam Prep

eAIN 51652

Foundations of Computer Science

Generally speaking, computer science is the study of computer technology, both hardware and software. However, computer science is a diverse field; the required skills are both applicable and in-demand across practically every industry in today's technology-dependent world.

:: Formal languages ::

A _____ is a mark, sign or word that indicates, signifies, or is understood as representing an idea, object, or relationship. _____ s allow people to go beyond what is known or seen by creating linkages between otherwise very different concepts and experiences. All communication is achieved through the use of _____ s. _____ s take the form of words, sounds, gestures, ideas or visual images and are used to convey other ideas and beliefs. For example, a red octagon may be a _____ for "STOP". On a map, a blue line might represent a river. Numerals are _____ s for numbers. Alphabetic letters may be _____ s for sounds. Personal names are _____ s representing individuals. A red rose may _____ ize love and compassion. The variable `x`, in a mathematical equation, may _____ ize the position of a particle in space.

Exam Probability: **Low**

1. *Answer choices:*

(see index for correct answer)

- a. Context-free language
- b. Attribute grammar
- c. Trace theory
- d. Symbol

Guidance: level 1

:: OS X email clients ::

The _____ or post is a system for physically transporting postcards, letters, and parcels. A postal service can be private or public, though many governments place restrictions on private systems. Since the mid-19th century, national postal systems have generally been established as government monopolies, with a fee on the article prepaid. Proof of payment is often in the form of adhesive postage stamps, but postage meters are also used for bulk _____ ing. Modern private postal systems are typically distinguished from national postal agencies by the names "courier" or "delivery service".

Exam Probability: **High**

2. *Answer choices:*

(see index for correct answer)

- a. GyazMail
- b. GroupWise
- c. Sparrow

Guidance: level 1

:: Music video games ::

_____ is an art form and cultural activity whose medium is sound organized in time. General definitions of _____ include common elements such as pitch , rhythm , dynamics , and the sonic qualities of timbre and texture . Different styles or types of _____ may emphasize, de-emphasize or omit some of these elements. _____ is performed with a vast range of instruments and vocal techniques ranging from singing to rapping; there are solely instrumental pieces, solely vocal pieces and pieces that combine singing and instruments. The word derives from Greek μς .See glossary of _____ al terminology.

Exam Probability: **Medium**

3. *Answer choices:*

(see index for correct answer)

- a. Music
- b. MusicVR
- c. Get On Da Mic
- d. Synthesia

Guidance: level 1

:: Graphical user interface elements ::

A _____ is an opening in a wall, door, roof or vehicle that allows the passage of light, sound, and air. Modern _____ s are usually glazed or covered in some other transparent or translucent material, a sash set in a frame in the opening; the sash and frame are also referred to as a _____ . Many glazed _____ s may be opened, to allow ventilation, or closed, to exclude inclement weather. _____ s often have a latch or similar mechanism to lock the _____ shut or to hold it open by various amounts.

Exam Probability: **Medium**

4. *Answer choices:*

(see index for correct answer)

- a. Pager
- b. Dialog box
- c. Window
- d. Tab

Guidance: level 1

:: System administration ::

A _____ is a system monitor program used to provide information about the processes and applications running on a computer, as well as the general status of the computer. Some implementations can also be used to terminate processes and applications, as well as change the processes' scheduling priority. In some environments, users can access a _____ with the Control-Alt-Delete keyboard shortcut.

5. *Answer choices:*

(see index for correct answer)

- a. Loginventory
- b. Microsoft Management Console
- c. Conversational Programming System
- d. Task manager

Guidance: level 1

:: Information science ::

A _____ is a written, drawn, presented, or memorialized representation of thought. a _____ is a form, or written piece that trains a line of thought or as in history, a significant event. The word originates from the Latin _____ um, which denotes a "teaching" or "lesson": the verb doceo denotes "to teach". In the past, the word was usually used to denote a written proof useful as evidence of a truth or fact. In the computer age, "_____" usually denotes a primarily textual computer file, including its structure and format, e.g. fonts, colors, and images. Contemporarily, "_____" is not defined by its transmission medium, e.g., paper, given the existence of electronic _____ s. "_____ ation" is distinct because it has more denotations than "_____". _____ s are also distinguished from "realia", which are three-dimensional objects that would otherwise satisfy the definition of "_____" because they memorialize or represent thought; _____ s are considered more as 2 dimensional representations. While _____ s are able to have large varieties of customization, all _____ s are able to be shared freely, and have the right to do so, creativity can be represented by _____ s, also. History, events, examples, opinion, etc. all can be expressed in _____ s.

Exam Probability: **High**

6. *Answer choices:*

(see index for correct answer)

- a. Investigative Data Warehouse
- b. Documentation science
- c. Informationist
- d. Document

Guidance: level 1

:: Computer memory ::

_____ , in contrast to non- _____ , is computer memory that requires power to maintain the stored information; it retains its contents while powered on but when the power is interrupted, the stored data is quickly lost.

Exam Probability: **High**

7. *Answer choices:*

(see index for correct answer)

- a. Volatile memory
- b. Core rope memory
- c. Video memory
- d. NVDIMM

Guidance: level 1

:: World Wide Web ::

The _____ , commonly known as the Web, is an information system where documents and other web resources are identified by Uniform Resource Locators , which may be interlinked by hypertext, and are accessible over the Internet. The resources of the WWW may be accessed by users by a software application called a web browser.

Exam Probability: **Low**

8. *Answer choices:*

- a. Web Medica Acreditada
- b. World Wide Web
- c. Linked data page
- d. Ovi

Guidance: level 1

:: Algorithm description languages ::

_____ is an informal high-level description of the operating principle of a computer program or other algorithm.

Exam Probability: **Low**

9. *Answer choices:*

- a. Pidgin code
- b. Structured English
- c. Program Design Language
- d. Pseudocode

Guidance: level 1

:: Network management ::

A _____ is the person designated in an organization whose responsibility includes maintaining computer infrastructures with emphasis on networking. Responsibilities may vary between organizations, but on-site servers, software-network interactions as well as network integrity/resilience are the key areas of focus.

Exam Probability: **Medium**

10. *Answer choices:*

(see index for correct answer)

- a. EADAS
- b. Digital data systems
- c. Fault management
- d. Network administrator

Guidance: level 1

:: Cloud infrastructure ::

_____ is the on-demand availability of computer system resources, especially data storage and computing power, without direct active management by the user. The term is generally used to describe data centers available to many users over the Internet. Large clouds, predominant today, often have functions distributed over multiple locations from central servers. If the connection to the user is relatively close, it may be designated an edge server.

Exam Probability: **High**

11. *Answer choices:*

(see index for correct answer)

- a. Animoto
- b. Cloudian, Inc.
- c. Software-defined data center
- d. TurnKey Linux Virtual Appliance Library

Guidance: level 1

:: Computer file systems ::

In computing, _____ code or an _____ file or _____ program, sometimes simply referred to as an _____ , causes a computer "to perform indicated tasks according to encoded instructions", as opposed to a data file that must be parsed by a program to be meaningful.

Exam Probability: **Medium**

12. *Answer choices:*

(see index for correct answer)

- a. Executable
- b. Linear Tape File System
- c. Cylinder-head-sector
- d. DLLM .NET Framework

Guidance: level 1

:: Mechanical computers ::

The _____ was a proposed mechanical general-purpose computer designed by English mathematician and computer pioneer Charles Babbage. It was first described in 1837 as the successor to Babbage's difference engine, a design for a simpler mechanical computer.

Exam Probability: **Low**

13. *Answer choices:*

(see index for correct answer)

- a. Ball-and-disk integrator
- b. Z1
- c. Dr. NIM
- d. Analytical Engine

:: Mathematical logic ::

_____ is an arrangement and organization of interrelated elements in a material object or system, or the object or system so organized. Material _____ s include man-made objects such as buildings and machines and natural objects such as biological organisms, minerals and chemicals. Abstract _____ s include data _____ s in computer science and musical form. Types of _____ include a hierarchy , a network featuring many-to-many links, or a lattice featuring connections between components that are neighbors in space.

Exam Probability: **Medium**

14. *Answer choices:*

(see index for correct answer)

- a. Structure
- b. Turnstile
- c. Notre Dame Journal of Formal Logic
- d. Logical machine

:: History of the Internet ::

The _____ is a standard network protocol used for the transfer of computer files between a client and server on a computer network.

Exam Probability: **Low**

15. *Answer choices:*

- a. EPpy Awards
- b. File Transfer Protocol
- c. Persistent uniform resource locator
- d. Internet in a Box

Guidance: level 1

:: Character encoding ::

_____ is a computing industry standard for the consistent encoding, representation, and handling of text expressed in most of the world's writing systems. The standard is maintained by the _____ Consortium, and as of May 2019 the most recent version, _____ 12.1, contains a repertoire of 137,994 characters covering 150 modern and historic scripts, as well as multiple symbol sets and emoji. The character repertoire of the _____ Standard is synchronized with ISO/IEC 10646, and both are code-for-code identical.

Exam Probability: **Low**

16. *Answer choices:*

(see index for correct answer)

- a. Variable-width encoding
- b. UTF-8
- c. UTF-32
- d. Transcode

Guidance: level 1

:: Concepts in logic ::

A _____ is a term used for identification. _____ s can identify a class or category of things, or a single thing, either uniquely, or within a given context. The entity identified by a _____ is called its referent. A personal _____ identifies, not necessarily uniquely, a specific individual human. The _____ of a specific entity is sometimes called a proper _____ and is, when consisting of only one word, a proper noun. Other nouns are sometimes called "common _____ s" or "general _____ s". A _____ can be given to a person, place, or thing; for example, parents can give their child a _____ or a scientist can give an element a _____ .

Exam Probability: **High**

17. *Answer choices:*

(see index for correct answer)

- a. Explanandum

- b. Supertask
- c. Truth
- d. Name

Guidance: level 1

:: Microsoft Windows file system technology ::

In computing, `<code> _____ </code>`, a command-line utility included in 86-DOS, MS-DOS, IBM PC DOS and OS/2, Microsoft Windows and ReactOS operating systems, carries out disk _____ ting.

Exam Probability: **Medium**

18. *Answer choices:*

(see index for correct answer)

- a. Powercfg
- b. W32tm
- c. Long filename
- d. Convert

Guidance: level 1

:: Formal languages ::

In computer text processing, a _____ is a system for annotating a document in a way that is syntactically distinguishable from the text. The idea and terminology evolved from the "marking up" of paper manuscripts, i.e., the revision instructions by editors, traditionally written with a red or blue pencil on authors' manuscripts. In digital media this "blue pencil instruction text" was replaced by tags, which indicate what the parts of the document are, rather than details of how they might be shown on some display. This lets authors avoid formatting every instance of the same kind of thing redundantly . It also avoids the specification of fonts and dimensions, which may not apply to many users .

Exam Probability: **Low**

19. *Answer choices:*

(see index for correct answer)

- a. Splicing rule
- b. Markup language
- c. Stochastic language
- d. Range concatenation grammars

Guidance: level 1

:: Network architecture ::

_____ is the design of a computer network. It is a framework for the specification of a network's physical components and their functional organization and configuration, its operational principles and procedures, as well as communication protocols used.

20. *Answer choices:*

(see index for correct answer)

- a. Network architecture
- b. Overlay network
- c. Infranet
- d. Open-access network

Guidance: level 1

:: Mac OS ::

The family of Macintosh operating systems developed by Apple Inc. includes the graphical user interface-based operating systems it has designed for use with its Macintosh series of personal computers since 1984, as well as the related system software it once created for compatible third-party systems.

Exam Probability: **Medium**

21. *Answer choices:*

(see index for correct answer)

- a. Old World ROM
- b. Mac OS
- c. Monaco

- d. System Information

:: Grid computing ::

_____ is the use of widely distributed computer resources to reach a common goal. A computing grid can be thought of as a distributed system with non-interactive workloads that involve a large number of files. _____ is distinguished from conventional high-performance computing systems such as cluster computing in that grid computers have each node set to perform a different task/application. Grid computers also tend to be more heterogeneous and geographically dispersed than cluster computers. Although a single grid can be dedicated to a particular application, commonly a grid is used for a variety of purposes. Grids are often constructed with general-purpose grid middleware software libraries. Grid sizes can be quite large.

Exam Probability: **Low**

22. *Answer choices:*

(see index for correct answer)

- a. Job Submission Description Language
- b. Grid computing
- c. Web Services Distributed Management
- d. Joint Battlespace Infosphere

:: Malware ::

_____ s or pop-ups are forms of online advertising on the World Wide Web. A pop-up is a graphical user interface display area, usually a small window, that suddenly appears in the foreground of the visual interface. The pop-up window containing an advertisement is usually generated by JavaScript that uses cross-site scripting, sometimes with a secondary payload that uses Adobe Flash. They can also be generated by other vulnerabilities/security holes in browser security.

Exam Probability: **Low**

23. *Answer choices:*

(see index for correct answer)

- a. Mahdi
- b. Typhoid adware
- c. Micro Bill Systems
- d. Polymorphic code

Guidance: level 1

:: Desktop publishing software ::

_____ is the creation of documents using page layout software on a personal computer. It was first used almost exclusively for print publications, but now it also assists in the creation of various forms of online content. _____ software can generate layouts and produce typographic-quality text and images comparable to traditional typography and printing. _____ is also the main reference for digital typography. This technology allows individuals, businesses, and other organizations to self-publish a wide variety of content, from menus to magazines to books, without the expense of commercial printing.

Exam Probability: **High**

24. *Answer choices:*

(see index for correct answer)

- a. XTension
- b. GeoPublish
- c. Adobe FrameMaker
- d. Desktop publishing

Guidance: level 1

:: Virtual reality ::

_____ is an experience taking place within simulated and immersive environments that can be similar to or completely different from the real world. Applications of _____ can include entertainment and educational purposes . Other, distinct types of VR style technology include augmented reality and mixed reality.

25. *Answer choices:*

(see index for correct answer)

- a. Virtual reality
- b. Virtual Reality and Education Laboratory
- c. Virtual war
- d. Unigine

Guidance: level 1

:: Computer network security ::

A _____ is an application which controls network traffic to and from a computer, permitting or denying communications based on a security policy. Typically it works as an application layer firewall.

Exam Probability: **Medium**

26. *Answer choices:*

(see index for correct answer)

- a. Fortinet
- b. Festi botnet
- c. Netsniff-ng
- d. Personal firewall

:: Data management ::

_____ is an object-oriented program and library developed by CERN. It was originally designed for particle physics data analysis and contains several features specific to this field, but it is also used in other applications such as astronomy and data mining. The latest release is 6.16.00, as of 2018-11-14.

Exam Probability: **Low**

27. *Answer choices:*

(see index for correct answer)

- a. Data stream management system
- b. World Wide Molecular Matrix
- c. DMAPI
- d. ROOT

:: Virtual reality ::

An _____ , also called an internet community or web community, is a virtual community whose members interact with each other primarily via the Internet. For many, online communities may feel like home, consisting of a "family of invisible friends". Those who wish to be a part of an _____ usually have to become a member via a specific site and thereby gain access to specific content or links. An _____ can act as an information system where members can post, comment on discussions, give advice or collaborate. Commonly, people communicate through social networking sites, chat rooms, forums, e-mail lists and discussion boards. People may also join online communities through video games, blogs and virtual worlds. The rise in popularity of Web 2.0 websites has allowed for easier real-time communication and ability to connect to others as well as producing new ways for information to be exchanged.

Exam Probability: **High**

28. *Answer choices:*

(see index for correct answer)

- a. Cyberwar
- b. Unigine
- c. Virtual world
- d. SixthSense

Guidance: level 1

:: Network protocols ::

In telecommunication, a communication protocol is a system of rules that allow two or more entities of a communications system to transmit information via any kind of variation of a physical quantity. The protocol defines the rules, syntax, semantics and synchronization of communication and possible error recovery methods. Protocols may be implemented by hardware, software, or a combination of both.

Exam Probability: **High**

29. *Answer choices:*

(see index for correct answer)

- a. Communications protocol
- b. TZSP
- c. MambaNet
- d. Windows Rally

Guidance: level 1

:: Photo software ::

_____ is a raster graphics editor developed and published by Adobe Inc. for Windows and macOS. It was originally created in 1988 by Thomas and John Knoll. Since then, this software has become the industry standard not only in raster graphics editing, but in digital art as a whole. The software's name has thus become a generic trademark, leading to its usage as a verb although Adobe discourages such use. Photoshop can edit and compose raster images in multiple layers and supports masks, alpha compositing, and several color models including RGB, CMYK, CIELAB, spot color, and duotone. Photoshop uses its own <code>PSD</code> and <code>PSB</code> file formats to support these features. In addition to raster graphics, this software has limited abilities to edit or render text and vector graphics , as well as 3D graphics and video. Its feature set can be expanded by plug-ins; programs developed and distributed independently of Photoshop that run inside it and offer new or enhanced features.

Exam Probability: **Low**

30. *Answer choices:*

(see index for correct answer)

- a. Process
- b. Hipstamatic
- c. Adobe Photoshop
- d. DxO Labs

Guidance: level 1

:: Teletraffic ::

A _____ is a connection over a telephone network between the called party and the calling party.

31. *Answer choices:*

(see index for correct answer)

- a. Call processing
- b. Demand assignment
- c. Busy-hour call attempts
- d. Least-cost routing

Guidance: level 1

:: Artificial intelligence ::

In artificial intelligence, an _____ is a computer system that emulates the decision-making ability of a human expert. _____ s are designed to solve complex problems by reasoning through bodies of knowledge, represented mainly as if–then rules rather than through conventional procedural code. The first _____ s were created in the 1970s and then proliferated in the 1980s. _____ s were among the first truly successful forms of artificial intelligence software. However, some experts point out that _____ s were not part of true artificial intelligence since they lack the ability to learn autonomously from external data. An _____ is divided into two subsystems: the inference engine and the knowledge base. The knowledge base represents facts and rules. The inference engine applies the rules to the known facts to deduce new facts. Inference engines can also include explanation and debugging abilities.

Exam Probability: **Medium**

32. *Answer choices:*

(see index for correct answer)

- a. ACROSS Project
- b. LIDA
- c. Zeuthen strategy
- d. Expert system

Guidance: level 1

:: ARM operating systems ::

_____ is a discontinued mobile operating system initially developed by Palm, Inc., for personal digital assistants in 1996. _____ was designed for ease of use with a touchscreen-based graphical user interface. It is provided with a suite of basic applications for personal information management. Later versions of the OS have been extended to support smartphones. Several other licensees have manufactured devices powered by _____.

Exam Probability: **Low**

33. *Answer choices:*

(see index for correct answer)

- a. OpenComRTOS
- b. Palm OS
- c. Android
- d. NCOS

Guidance: level 1

:: Application layer protocols ::

An _____ is an abstraction layer that specifies the shared communications protocols and interface methods used by hosts in a communications network. The _____ abstraction is used in both of the standard models of computer networking: the Internet Protocol Suite and the OSI model. Although both models use the same term for their respective highest level layer, the detailed definitions and purposes are different.

34. *Answer choices:*

(see index for correct answer)

- a. WebNFS
- b. MIMIC Simulator
- c. Wireless Communications Transfer Protocol
- d. Wire protocol

Guidance: level 1

:: Knowledge representation ::

In general usage, a _____ is a reference work that lists words grouped together according to similarity of meaning , in contrast to a dictionary, which provides definitions for words, and generally lists them in alphabetical order. The main purpose of such reference works for users "to find the word, or words, by which [an] idea may be most fitly and aptly expressed," quoting Peter Mark Roget, author of Roget`s _____ .

35. *Answer choices:*

(see index for correct answer)

- a. Defeasible reasoning
- b. Knowledge value chain

- c. Thesaurus
- d. Living graph

Guidance: level 1

:: Graphical user interface elements ::

The _____ is a graphical control element in the form of a small window that communicates information to the user and prompts them for a response.

Exam Probability: **High**

36. *Answer choices:*

(see index for correct answer)

- a. Address bar
- b. Title bar
- c. Shelf
- d. Dialog box

Guidance: level 1

:: Metropolitan area networks ::

_____ is a family of wireless broadband communication standards based on the IEEE 802.16 set of standards, which provide multiple physical layer and Media Access Control options.

Exam Probability: **Medium**

37. *Answer choices:*

(see index for correct answer)

- a. Local Multipoint Distribution Service
- b. WiMAX MIMO
- c. WiMAX
- d. Metro Ethernet

Guidance: level 1

:: Distributed computing architecture ::

The _____ is a standard for distributed simulation, used when building a simulation for a larger purpose by combining several simulations. The standard was developed in the 90's under the leadership of the US Department of Defense and was later transitioned to become an open international IEEE standard. It is a recommended standard within NATO through STANAG 4603. Today the HLA is used in a number of domains including defense and security and civilian applications. The architecture specifies the following components.

Exam Probability: **High**

38. *Answer choices:*

- a. Message consumer
- b. SIMPL
- c. High-level architecture
- d. Explicit multi-threading

Guidance: level 1

:: Internet Protocol ::

The _____ is the principal communications protocol in the _____ suite for relaying datagrams across network boundaries. Its routing function enables internetworking, and essentially establishes the Internet.

Exam Probability: **Medium**

39. *Answer choices:*

- a. IP Network Transformation
- b. IP in IP
- c. Internet Stream Protocol
- d. TCP/IP stack fingerprinting

Guidance: level 1

:: World Wide Web ::

_____ LLC is an American multinational technology company that specializes in Internet-related services and products, which include online advertising technologies, search engine, cloud computing, software, and hardware. It is considered one of the Big Four technology companies, alongside Amazon, Apple and Facebook.

Exam Probability: **Medium**

40. *Answer choices:*

(see index for correct answer)

- a. Web Single Sign-On Metadata Exchange Protocol
- b. Spamdexing
- c. DeepPeep
- d. Google

Guidance: level 1

:: Computer file systems ::

In computing, a _____ or filesystem controls how data is stored and retrieved. Without a _____ , information placed in a storage medium would be one large body of data with no way to tell where one piece of information stops and the next begins. By separating the data into pieces and giving each piece a name, the information is easily isolated and identified. Taking its name from the way paper-based information systems are named, each group of data is called a "file". The structure and logic rules used to manage the groups of information and their names is called a " _____ ".

Exam Probability: **High**

41. *Answer choices:*

(see index for correct answer)

- a. Apple Partition Map
- b. Common filesystem features
- c. Virtual Storage Access Method
- d. Compact Disc File System

Guidance: level 1

:: Computer storage media ::

Blu-ray or _____ is a digital optical disc data storage format. It was designed to supersede the DVD format, and is capable of storing several hours of video in high-definition and ultra high-definition resolution . The main application of Blu-ray is as a medium for video material such as feature films and for the physical distribution of video games for the PlayStation 3, PlayStation 4, and Xbox One. The name "Blu-ray" refers to the blue laser used to read the disc, which allows information to be stored at a greater density than is possible with the longer-wavelength red laser used for DVDs.

Exam Probability: **Medium**

42. *Answer choices:*

(see index for correct answer)

- a. Blu-ray Disc
- b. Removable media
- c. Paper disc
- d. LabelFlash

Guidance: level 1

:: Data structures ::

In computer science, a _____ is a data organization, management, and storage format that enables efficient access and modification. More precisely, a _____ is a collection of data values, the relationships among them, and the functions or operations that can be applied to the data.

43. *Answer choices:*

(see index for correct answer)

- a. Randomized meldable heap
- b. Disjoint-set data structure
- c. Succinct data structure
- d. Data structure

Guidance: level 1

:: GUI widgets ::

A _____ is a piece of paper, plastic film, cloth, metal, or other material affixed to a container or product, on which is written or printed information or symbols about the product or item. Information printed directly on a container or article can also be considered _____ ing.

Exam Probability: **Medium**

44. *Answer choices:*

(see index for correct answer)

- a. Label
- b. Progress bar
- c. Edit menu

- d. Infobar

Guidance: level 1

:: Formal methods ::

A _____ is a mathematical model of computation that defines an abstract machine, which manipulates symbols on a strip of tape according to a table of rules. Despite the model's simplicity, given any computer algorithm, a _____ capable of simulating that algorithm's logic can be constructed.

Exam Probability: **Low**

45. *Answer choices:*

(see index for correct answer)

- a. Turing machine
- b. Predicative programming
- c. Automated theorem proving
- d. Production equipment control

Guidance: level 1

:: Internet Protocol ::

In computer networking, the _____ is the lowest layer in the Internet Protocol Suite, the networking architecture of the Internet. It is described in RFC 1122 and RFC 1123. The _____ is the group of methods and communications protocols that only operate on the link that a host is physically connected to. The link is the physical and logical network component used to interconnect hosts or nodes in the network and a link protocol is a suite of methods and standards that operate only between adjacent network nodes of a local area network segment or a wide area network connection.

Exam Probability: **High**

46. *Answer choices:*

(see index for correct answer)

- a. IPv4
- b. IP in IP
- c. Access network discovery and selection function
- d. Link layer

Guidance: level 1

:: Cloud computing providers ::

_____ , Inc. was an American company that sold computers, computer components, software, and information technology services and created the Java programming language, the Solaris operating system, ZFS, the Network File System , and SPARC. Sun contributed significantly to the evolution of several key computing technologies, among them Unix, RISC processors, thin client computing, and virtualized computing. Sun was founded on February 24, 1982. At its height, the Sun headquarters were in Santa Clara, California , on the former west campus of the Agnews Developmental Center.

Exam Probability: **High**

47. *Answer choices:*

(see index for correct answer)

- a. Peer 1
- b. Skytap
- c. Sun Microsystems
- d. Autonomy Corporation

Guidance: level 1

:: Transaction processing ::

_____ is the maintenance of, and the assurance of the accuracy and consistency of, data over its entire life-cycle, and is a critical aspect to the design, implementation and usage of any system which stores, processes, or retrieves data. The term is broad in scope and may have widely different meanings depending on the specific context even under the same general umbrella of computing. It is at times used as a proxy term for data quality, while data validation is a pre-requisite for _____ . _____ is the opposite of data corruption. The overall intent of any _____ technique is the same: ensure data is recorded exactly as intended and upon later retrieval, ensure the data is the same as it was when it was originally recorded. In short, _____ aims to prevent unintentional changes to information. _____ is not to be confused with data security, the discipline of protecting data from unauthorized parties.

Exam Probability: **Medium**

48. *Answer choices:*

(see index for correct answer)

- a. Atomic commit
- b. Error account
- c. Data integrity
- d. Blind write

Guidance: level 1

:: Healthcare software ::

The Veterans Information Systems and Technology Architecture is the nationwide veterans clinical and business information system of the U.S. Department of Veterans Affairs. _____ consists of 180 applications for clinical, financial, and administrative functions all integrated within a single database, providing single, authoritative source of data for all veteran-related care and services. The U.S. Congress mandates the VA keep the veterans health record in a single, authoritative, lifelong database, which is _____ .

Exam Probability: **Medium**

49. *Answer choices:*

(see index for correct answer)

- a. VistA
- b. GlobeStar Systems
- c. PsyScope
- d. One-e-App

Guidance: level 1

:: Computing input devices ::

In computing, an _____ is a piece of computer hardware equipment used to provide data and control signals to an information processing system such as a computer or information appliance. Examples of _____ s include keyboards, mouse, scanners, digital cameras and joysticks. Audio _____ s may be used for purposes including speech recognition. Many companies are utilizing speech recognition to help assist users to use their device.

50. *Answer choices:*

(see index for correct answer)

- a. Project Digits
- b. Digital pen
- c. Input device
- d. Pointing device

Guidance: level 1

:: Operating systems ::

An _____ is system software that manages computer hardware and software resources and provides common services for computer programs.

51. *Answer choices:*

(see index for correct answer)

- a. Operating system
- b. Comparison of operating systems
- c. Operating System Patcher
- d. XB Machine

:: Software licenses ::

_____ is a type of proprietary software which is initially provided free of charge to users, who are allowed and encouraged to make and share copies of the program. _____ is often offered as a download from a website or as a compact disc included with a magazine. _____ is available with most computer software. _____ differs from open-source software, in which the source code is available for anyone to inspect and alter; and freeware, which is software distributed at no cost to the user but without source code being made available.

Exam Probability: **Medium**

52. *Answer choices:*

(see index for correct answer)

- a. Aladdin Free Public License
- b. T-License
- c. Software license
- d. Certificate of authenticity

:: World Wide Web Consortium standards ::

Hypertext Markup Language is the standard markup language for creating web pages and web applications. With Cascading Style Sheets and JavaScript, it forms a triad of cornerstone technologies for the World Wide Web.

Exam Probability: **Low**

53. *Answer choices:*

(see index for correct answer)

- a. XProc
- b. Cross-origin resource sharing
- c. Message Transmission Optimization Mechanism
- d. HTML

Guidance: level 1

:: Computing input devices ::

A _____ is a computer input device that enables a user to hand-draw images, animations and graphics, with a special pen-like stylus, similar to the way a person draws images with a pencil and paper. These tablets may also be used to capture data or handwritten signatures. It can also be used to trace an image from a piece of paper which is taped or otherwise secured to the tablet surface. Capturing data in this way, by tracing or entering the corners of linear poly-lines or shapes, is called digitizing.

Exam Probability: **Low**

54. *Answer choices:*

(see index for correct answer)

- a. Frame grabber
- b. Graphics tablet
- c. Controller-free motion control
- d. Mousepad

Guidance: level 1

:: Files ::

A _____ in computers is a critical computer file without which a computer system may not operate correctly. These files may come as part of the operating system, a third-party device driver or other sources. Microsoft Windows and MS-DOS mark their more valuable _____ s with a "system" attribute to protect them against accidental deletion.

Exam Probability: **Low**

55. *Answer choices:*

(see index for correct answer)

- a. JHOVE
- b. End-of-file
- c. Scratch space
- d. Zero byte file

:: SCSI ::

Small Computer System Interface is a set of standards for physically connecting and transferring data between computers and peripheral devices. The _____ standards define commands, protocols, electrical, optical and logical interfaces. _____ is most commonly used for hard disk drives and tape drives, but it can connect a wide range of other devices, including scanners and CD drives, although not all controllers can handle all devices. The _____ standard defines command sets for specific peripheral device types; the presence of "unknown" as one of these types means that in theory it can be used as an interface to almost any device, but the standard is highly pragmatic and addressed toward commercial requirements.

Exam Probability: **Medium**

56. *Answer choices:*

(see index for correct answer)

- a. USB Attached SCSI
- b. SCSI Request Sense Command
- c. SCSI Read Capacity Command
- d. SCSI Pass Through Interface

:: System software ::

_____ is software designed to provide a platform for other software. Examples of _____ include operating systems like macOS, Ubuntu and Microsoft Windows, computational science software, game engines, industrial automation, and software as a service applications.

Exam Probability: **Medium**

57. *Answer choices:*

(see index for correct answer)

- a. Verdiem
- b. System software
- c. PowerMAN
- d. ManageEngine AssetExplorer

Guidance: level 1

:: Bioinformatics software ::

_____ is a free online bioinformatics resource developed by the Laboratory of Immunopathogenesis and Bioinformatics . All tools in the _____ Bioinformatics Resources aim to provide functional interpretation of large lists of genes derived from genomic studies, e.g. microarray and proteomics studies. _____ can be found at http:// _____ .niaid.nih.gov or http:// _____ .abcc.ncifcrf.gov

Exam Probability: **High**

58. *Answer choices:*

(see index for correct answer)

- a. PDBREPORT
- b. PHYLIP
- c. DAVID
- d. PrimerPlex

Guidance: level 1

:: Infographics ::

A _____ is a symbolic representation of information according to visualization technique. _____ s have been used since ancient times, but became more prevalent during the Enlightenment. Sometimes, the technique uses a three-dimensional visualization which is then projected onto a two-dimensional surface. The word graph is sometimes used as a synonym for _____ .

Exam Probability: **Medium**

59. *Answer choices:*

(see index for correct answer)

- a. Diagram
- b. Information sign
- c. Placard
- d. Strategy visualization

Guidance: level 1

Computers

A computer is a device that can be instructed to carry out sequences of arithmetic or logical operations automatically via computer programming. Modern computers have the ability to follow generalized sets of operations, called programs. These programs enable computers to perform an extremely wide range of tasks.

:: Firewall software ::

_____ , is a firewall component of Microsoft Windows. It was first included in Windows XP and Windows Server 2003. Prior to the release of Windows XP Service Pack 2 in 2004, it was known as Internet Connection Firewall. With the release of Windows 10 version 1709, in September 2017, it was renamed Windows Defender Firewall as part of the "Windows Defender" branding campaign.

Exam Probability: **Low**

1. *Answer choices:*

(see index for correct answer)

- a. Windows Firewall
- b. Kerio Technologies
- c. Matousec
- d. IPFire

Guidance: level 1

:: Digital circuits ::

_____ is the length of time taken for the quantity of interest to reach its destination. It can relate to networking, electronics or physics.

Exam Probability: **Medium**

2. *Answer choices:*

(see index for correct answer)

- a. Propagation delay
- b. Digital timing diagram
- c. Binary multiplier
- d. Encoder

Guidance: level 1

:: Classes of computers ::

A _____ was a computer designed to be easily moved from one place to another and included a display and keyboard. The first commercially sold portable was the 50 pound IBM 5100, introduced 1975. The next major portables were Osborne's 24 pound CP/M-based Osborne 1 and Compaq's 28 pound 100% IBM PC compatible Compaq Portable . These "luggable" computers lacked the next technological development, not requiring an external power source; that feature was introduced by the laptop. Laptops were followed by lighter models, so that in the 2000s mobile devices and by 2007 smartphones made the term almost meaningless. The 2010s introduced wearable computers such as smartwatches.

Exam Probability: **Medium**

3. *Answer choices:*

(see index for correct answer)

- a. Legacy-free PC
- b. Portable computer
- c. Minimalism
- d. Topological quantum computer

Guidance: level 1

:: Packet radio ::

_____ is a digital radio communications mode used to send packets of data. _____ uses packet switching to transmit datagrams. This is very similar to how packets of data are transferred between nodes on the Internet. _____ can be used to transmit data long distances.

Exam Probability: **Medium**

4. *Answer choices:*

- a. FBB
- b. Turbo Dispatch
- c. Packet radio
- d. PSK63

Guidance: level 1

:: Holism ::

In computer programming, a _____ is a sequence of program instructions that performs a specific task, packaged as a unit. This unit can then be used in programs wherever that particular task should be performed.

Exam Probability: **Medium**

5. *Answer choices:*

- a. Subroutine
- b. Integral ecology
- c. Two Dogmas of Empiricism
- d. Complexity

Guidance: level 1

:: Digital circuits ::

An _____ is a combinational digital electronic circuit that performs arithmetic and bitwise operations on integer binary numbers. This is in contrast to a floating-point unit , which operates on floating point numbers. An ALU is a fundamental building block of many types of computing circuits, including the central processing unit of computers, FPUs, and graphics processing units . A single CPU, FPU or GPU may contain multiple ALUs.

Exam Probability: **High**

6. *Answer choices:*
(see index for correct answer)

- a. Boolean circuit
- b. Address decoder
- c. Wallace tree
- d. Arithmetic logic unit

Guidance: level 1

:: Software ::

Computer _____ , or simply _____ , is a collection of data or computer instructions that tell the computer how to work. This is in contrast to physical hardware, from which the system is built and actually performs the work. In computer science and _____ engineering, computer _____ is all information processed by computer systems, programs and data. Computer _____ includes computer programs, libraries and related non-executable data, such as online documentation or digital media. Computer hardware and _____ require each other and neither can be realistically used on its own.

Exam Probability: **High**

7. *Answer choices:*

(see index for correct answer)

- a. Xdvi
- b. Software
- c. Journal of Systems and Software
- d. Backlog

Guidance: level 1

:: Local area networks ::

A _____ is a computer network that interconnects computers within a limited area such as a residence, school, laboratory, university campus or office building. By contrast, a wide area network not only covers a larger geographic distance, but also generally involves leased telecommunication circuits.

Exam Probability: **Medium**

8. *Answer choices:*

(see index for correct answer)

- a. Fiber Distributed Data Interface
- b. Cambridge Ring
- c. Local area network
- d. Subinterface

Guidance: level 1

:: Infographics ::

A _____ is a type of diagram used in computer science and related fields to describe the behavior of systems. _____ s require that the system described is composed of a finite number of states; sometimes, this is indeed the case, while at other times this is a reasonable abstraction. Many forms of _____ s exist, which differ slightly and have different semantics.

Exam Probability: **Medium**

9. *Answer choices:*

(see index for correct answer)

- a. State diagram
- b. Wayfinding
- c. A Chart of Biography
- d. No symbol

Guidance: level 1

:: Embedded systems ::

A _____ , cell phone, cellphone, or hand phone, sometimes shortened to simply mobile, cell or just phone, is a portable telephone that can make and receive calls over a radio frequency link while the user is moving within a telephone service area. The radio frequency link establishes a connection to the switching systems of a _____ operator, which provides access to the public switched telephone network . Modern mobile telephone services use a cellular network architecture, and, therefore, mobile telephones are called cellular telephones or cell phones, in North America. In addition to telephony, 2000s-era _____ s support a variety of other services, such as text messaging, MMS, email, Internet access, short-range wireless communications , business applications, video games, and digital photography. _____ s offering only those capabilities are known as feature phones; _____ s which offer greatly advanced computing capabilities are referred to as smartphones.

Exam Probability: **Medium**

10. *Answer choices:*

(see index for correct answer)

- a. Sensor node
- b. Tektronix extended HEX
- c. Ceibo Emulators
- d. Mobile phone

Guidance: level 1

:: Computer memory form factor ::

A _____ , or single in-line memory module, is a type of memory module containing random-access memory used in computers from the early 1980s to the late 1990s. It differs from a dual in-line memory module , the most predominant form of memory module today, in that the contacts on a _____ are redundant on both sides of the module. _____ s were standardised under the JEDEC JESD-21C standard.

Exam Probability: **High**

11. *Answer choices:*
(see index for correct answer)

- a. AGP Inline Memory Module
- b. SIMM

Guidance: level 1

:: Clock signal ::

In computing _____ is the practice of increasing the clock frequency of a computer to exceed that certified by the manufacturer. Commonly operating voltage is also increased to maintain a component's operational stability at accelerated speeds. Semiconductor devices operated at higher frequencies and voltages increase power consumption and heat. An overclocked device may be unreliable or fail completely if the additional heat load is not removed or power delivery components cannot meet increased power demands. Many device warranties state that _____ and/or over-specification voids any warranty.

Exam Probability: **High**

12. *Answer choices:*

(see index for correct answer)

- a. Source-synchronous
- b. Clock gating
- c. Instructions per cycle
- d. Overclocking

Guidance: level 1

:: Instruction processing ::

A _____ is an agent which has the potential to cause harm to a vulnerable target. The terms " _____ " and "risk" are often used interchangeably. However, in terms of risk assessment, they are two very distinct terms. A _____ is any agent that can cause harm or damage to humans, property, or the environment. Risk is defined as the probability that exposure to a _____ will lead to a negative consequence, or more simply, a _____ poses no risk if there is no exposure to that _____ .

Exam Probability: **Low**

13. *Answer choices:*

(see index for correct answer)

- a. Operand forwarding
- b. Unicore
- c. Hazard
- d. Instruction cycle

Guidance: level 1

:: Data search engines ::

A web _____ or Internet _____ is a software system that is designed to carry out web search , which means to search the World Wide Web in a systematic way for particular information specified in a web search query. The search results are generally presented in a line of results, often referred to as _____ results pages . The information may be a mix of web pages, images, videos, infographics, articles, research papers and other types of files. Some _____ s also mine data available in databases or open directories. Unlike web directories, which are maintained only by human editors, _____ s also maintain real-time information by running an algorithm on a web crawler.Internet content that is not capable of being searched by a web _____ is generally described as the deep web.

Exam Probability: **Low**

14. *Answer choices:*

(see index for correct answer)

- a. Mugurdy
- b. Open Drive
- c. Search/Retrieve via URL
- d. Quandl

Guidance: level 1

:: Home automation ::

A _____ is a serial assembly of connected pieces, called links, typically made of metal, with an overall character similar to that of a rope in that it is flexible and curved in compression but linear, rigid, and load-bearing in tension. A _____ may consist of two or more links. _____ s can be classified by their design, which is dictated by their use.

Exam Probability: **High**

15. *Answer choices:*

- a. Tenrehte Technologies, Inc.
- b. Electronics Design Group
- c. HomeLink Wireless Control System
- d. Chain

Guidance: level 1

:: Character encoding ::

_____ is a computing industry standard for the consistent encoding, representation, and handling of text expressed in most of the world's writing systems. The standard is maintained by the _____ Consortium, and as of May 2019 the most recent version, _____ 12.1, contains a repertoire of 137,994 characters covering 150 modern and historic scripts, as well as multiple symbol sets and emoji. The character repertoire of the _____ Standard is synchronized with ISO/IEC 10646, and both are code-for-code identical.

16. *Answer choices:*

(see index for correct answer)

- a. Vietnamese Quoted-Readable
- b. World glyph set
- c. Baudot code
- d. Unicode

Guidance: level 1

:: Interrupts ::

In system programming, an _____ is a signal to the processor emitted by hardware or software indicating an event that needs immediate attention. An _____ alerts the processor to a high-priority condition requiring the _____ ion of the current code the processor is executing. The processor responds by suspending its current activities, saving its state, and executing a function called an _____ handler to deal with the event. This _____ ion is temporary, and, after the _____ handler finishes, the processor resumes normal activities. There are two types of _____ s: hardware _____ s and software _____ s .

Exam Probability: **Medium**

17. *Answer choices:*

(see index for correct answer)

- a. Interrupt coalescing
- b. End of interrupt
- c. Interrupt
- d. Interrupt storm

Guidance: level 1

:: Central processing unit ::

In computer engineering, _____ , also called computer organization and sometimes abbreviated as μarch or uarch, is the way a given instruction set architecture is implemented in a particular processor. A given ISA may be implemented with different _____ s; implementations may vary due to different goals of a given design or due to shifts in technology.

Exam Probability: **Medium**

18. *Answer choices:*
(see index for correct answer)

- a. Control register
- b. Microarchitecture
- c. Microcontroller
- d. Architectural state

Guidance: level 1

:: Computer buses ::

A _____ is a group of electrical connectors in parallel with each other, so that each pin of each connector is linked to the same relative pin of all the other connectors, forming a computer bus. It is used as a backbone to connect several printed circuit boards together to make up a complete computer system. _____ s commonly use a printed circuit board, but wire-wrapped _____ s have also been used in minicomputers and high-reliability applications.

Exam Probability: **High**

19. *Answer choices:*

(see index for correct answer)

- a. OpenVPX
- b. XCP
- c. JEIDA memory card
- d. Backplane

Guidance: level 1

:: Classes of computers ::

A _____ is a personal computer designed for regular use at a single location on or near a desk or table due to its size and power requirements. The most common configuration has a case that houses the power supply, motherboard , disk storage ; a keyboard and mouse for input; and a computer monitor, speakers, and, often, a printer for output. The case may be oriented horizontally or vertically and placed either underneath, beside, or on top of a desk.

Exam Probability: **Low**

20. *Answer choices:*

(see index for correct answer)

- a. Stored-program computer
- b. GRiDPad
- c. MISD
- d. SISD

Guidance: level 1

:: Desktop publishing software ::

_____ is the creation of documents using page layout software on a personal computer. It was first used almost exclusively for print publications, but now it also assists in the creation of various forms of online content. _____ software can generate layouts and produce typographic-quality text and images comparable to traditional typography and printing. _____ is also the main reference for digital typography. This technology allows individuals, businesses, and other organizations to self-publish a wide variety of content, from menus to magazines to books, without the expense of commercial printing.

Exam Probability: **High**

21. *Answer choices:*

(see index for correct answer)

- a. Fleet Street Publisher
- b. Desktop publishing
- c. Style sheet
- d. XTension

Guidance: level 1

:: Internet architecture ::

In computer networking, IntServ or _____ is an architecture that specifies the elements to guarantee quality of service on networks. IntServ can for example be used to allow video and sound to reach the receiver without interruption.

22. *Answer choices:*

(see index for correct answer)

- a. Resource Reservation Protocol
- b. Route Views
- c. QPPB
- d. Tier 1 network

Guidance: level 1

:: Computer architecture ::

The _____ is a computer architecture with physically separate storage and signal pathways for instructions and data. The term originated from the Harvard Mark I relay-based computer, which stored instructions on punched tape and data in electro-mechanical counters. These early machines had data storage entirely contained within the central processing unit, and provided no access to the instruction storage as data. Programs needed to be loaded by an operator; the processor could not initialize itself.

Exam Probability: **High**

23. *Answer choices:*

(see index for correct answer)

- a. Anykernel

- b. Harvard architecture
- c. Computer architecture simulator
- d. Stream processing

Guidance: level 1

:: Computer memory ::

_____ stands for electrically erasable programmable read-only memory and is a type of non-volatile memory used in computers, integrated in microcontrollers for smart cards and remote keyless systems, and other electronic devices to store relatively small amounts of data but allowing individual bytes to be erased and reprogrammed.

Exam Probability: **Low**

24. *Answer choices:*

(see index for correct answer)

- a. Cache on a stick
- b. External memory interface
- c. Base address
- d. Reprom

Guidance: level 1

:: Wireless networking ::

_____ communication, or sometimes simply _____ , is the transfer of information or power between two or more points that are not connected by an electrical conductor. The most common _____ technologies use radio waves. With radio waves distances can be short, such as a few meters for Bluetooth or as far as millions of kilometers for deep-space radio communications. It encompasses various types of fixed, mobile, and portable applications, including two-way radios, cellular telephones, personal digital assistants , and _____ networking. Other examples of applications of radio technology include GPS units, garage door openers, _____ computer mice, keyboards and headsets, headphones, radio receivers, satellite television, broadcast television and cordless telephones. Somewhat less common methods of achieving _____ communications include the use of other electromagnetic _____ technologies, such as light, magnetic, or electric fields or the use of sound.

Exam Probability: **Medium**

25. *Answer choices:*

(see index for correct answer)

- a. Wireless mesh network
- b. IQRF
- c. Ekahau Site Survey
- d. Wireless

Guidance: level 1

:: Malware ::

_____ is any software intentionally designed to cause damage to a computer, server, client, or computer network. _____ does the damage after it is implanted or introduced in some way into a target's computer and can take the form of executable code, scripts, active content, and other software. The code is described as computer viruses, worms, Trojan horses, ransomware, spyware, adware, and scareware, among other terms. _____ has a malicious intent, acting against the interest of the computer user—and so does not include software that causes unintentional harm due to some deficiency, which is typically described as a software bug.

Exam Probability: **Low**

26. *Answer choices:*

(see index for correct answer)

- a. Malware
- b. MonaRonaDona
- c. Anti-Malware Testing Standards Organization
- d. 3wPlayer

Guidance: level 1

:: Transport layer protocols ::

In computer networking, the _____ is a conceptual division of methods in the layered architecture of protocols in the network stack in the Internet protocol suite and the OSI model. The protocols of this layer provide host-to-host communication services for applications. It provides services such as connection-oriented communication, reliability, flow control, and multiplexing.

Exam Probability: **High**

27. *Answer choices:*

(see index for correct answer)

- a. Datagram Congestion Control Protocol
- b. Transport Layer
- c. Stream Control Transmission Protocol
- d. UDP Lite

Guidance: level 1

:: Data collection ::

A _____ is an utterance which typically functions as a request for information. _____ s can thus be understood as a kind of illocutionary act in the field of pragmatics or as special kinds of propositions in frameworks of formal semantics such as alternative semantics or inquisitive semantics. The information requested is expected to be provided in the form of an answer. _____ s are often conflated with interrogatives, which are the grammatical forms typically used to achieve them. Rhetorical _____ s, for example, are interrogative in form but may not be considered true _____ s as they are not expected to be answered. Conversely, non-interrogative grammatical structures may be considered _____ s as in the case of the imperative sentence "tell me your name".

Exam Probability: **High**

28. *Answer choices:*

(see index for correct answer)

- a. General Social Survey
- b. European social survey
- c. Guardian
- d. Question

Guidance: level 1

:: Digital typography ::

International Business Machines Corporation is an American multinational information technology company headquartered in Armonk, New York, with operations in over 170 countries. The company began in 1911, founded in Endicott, New York, as the Computing-Tabulating-Recording Company and was renamed "International Business Machines" in 1924.

Exam Probability: **Low**

29. *Answer choices:*

(see index for correct answer)

- a. TeX font metric
- b. HarfBuzz
- c. IBM
- d. Adobe Font Folio

Guidance: level 1

:: Debuggers ::

_____ is the process of finding and resolving defects or problems within a computer program that prevent correct operation of computer software or a system.

Exam Probability: **High**

30. *Answer choices:*

(see index for correct answer)

- a. Debugging
- b. Debugger
- c. Remedy Debugger
- d. Microsoft Visual Studio Debugger

Guidance: level 1

:: File sharing networks ::

_____ computing or networking is a distributed application architecture that partitions tasks or workloads between peers. Peers are equally privileged, equipotent participants in the application. They are said to form a _____ network of nodes.

Exam Probability: **Medium**

31. *Answer choices:*

(see index for correct answer)

- a. Proxyshare
- b. Direct Connect
- c. Peer-to-peer
- d. Peersites

Guidance: level 1

:: Classes of computers ::

A _____ , or colloquially mini, is a class of smaller computers that was developed in the mid-1960s and sold for much less than mainframe and mid-size computers from IBM and its direct competitors. In a 1970 survey, The New York Times suggested a consensus definition of a _____ as a machine costing less than US$25,000 , with an input-output device such as a teleprinter and at least four thousand words of memory, that is capable of running programs in a higher level language, such as Fortran or BASIC. The class formed a distinct group with its own software architectures and operating systems. Minis were designed for control, instrumentation, human interaction, and communication switching as distinct from calculation and record keeping. Many were sold indirectly to original equipment manufacturers for final end use application. During the two decade lifetime of the _____ class , almost 100 companies formed and only a half dozen remained.

Exam Probability: **Medium**

32. *Answer choices:*

(see index for correct answer)

- a. Minicomputer
- b. Chaos computing
- c. Membrane computing
- d. Plessey System 250

Guidance: level 1

:: Central processing unit ::

A _____ is a collection of functional units such as arithmetic logic units or multipliers, that perform data processing operations, registers, and buses. Along with the control unit it composes the central processing unit .. A larger _____ can be made by joining more than one number of _____ s using multiplexer.

Exam Probability: **Medium**

33. *Answer choices:*

(see index for correct answer)

- a. Dynamic frequency scaling
- b. Microarchitecture
- c. Berkeley RISC
- d. Datapath

Guidance: level 1

:: Operating systems ::

An _____ is system software that manages computer hardware and software resources and provides common services for computer programs.

Exam Probability: **High**

34. *Answer choices:*

(see index for correct answer)

- a. LIO Target
- b. Catamount
- c. Operating system
- d. PUD

Guidance: level 1

:: Logic gates ::

In digital electronics, a _____ is a logic gate which produces an output which is false only if all its inputs are true; thus its output is complement to that of an AND gate. A LOW output results only if all the inputs to the gate are HIGH ; if any input is LOW , a HIGH output results. A _____ is made using transistors and junction diodes. By De Morgan's theorem, a two-input _____ 's logic may be expressed as AB=A+B, making a _____ equivalent to inverters followed by an OR gate.

Exam Probability: **Medium**

35. *Answer choices:*

(see index for correct answer)

- a. or gate
- b. nor gate
- c. xnor gate
- d. xor gate

:: Digital circuits ::

A _____ is a circuit or algorithm that compresses multiple binary inputs into a smaller number of outputs. The output of a _____ is the binary representation of the original number starting from zero of the most significant input bit. They are often used to control interrupt requests by acting on the highest _____ .

Exam Probability: **Low**

36. *Answer choices:*

(see index for correct answer)

- a. Lookahead carry unit
- b. Priority encoder
- c. Address decoder
- d. Boolean circuit

:: Distributed computing architecture ::

The _____ is a standard for distributed simulation, used when building a simulation for a larger purpose by combining several simulations. The standard was developed in the 90's under the leadership of the US Department of Defense and was later transitioned to become an open international IEEE standard. It is a recommended standard within NATO through STANAG 4603. Today the HLA is used in a number of domains including defense and security and civilian applications. The architecture specifies the following components.

Exam Probability: **Low**

37. *Answer choices:*

(see index for correct answer)

- a. Dryad
- b. Live distributed object
- c. High-level architecture
- d. Aggregate Level Simulation Protocol

Guidance: level 1

:: Automatic identification and data capture ::

A _____ is a visual, machine-readable representation of data; the data usually describes something about the object that carries the _____ . Traditional _____ s systematically represent data by varying the widths and spacings of parallel lines, and may be referred to as linear or one-dimensional . Later, two-dimensional variants were developed, using rectangles, dots, hexagons and other geometric patterns, called matrix codes or 2D _____ s, although they do not use bars as such. Initially, _____ s were only scanned by special optical scanners called _____ readers. Later application software became available for devices that could read images, such as smartphones with cameras.

Exam Probability: **Low**

38. *Answer choices:*

(see index for correct answer)

- a. Guard tour patrol system
- b. Automatic equipment identification
- c. Automated species identification
- d. Impinj

Guidance: level 1

:: Bioinformatics software ::

_____ is a free online bioinformatics resource developed by the Laboratory of Immunopathogenesis and Bioinformatics . All tools in the _____ Bioinformatics Resources aim to provide functional interpretation of large lists of genes derived from genomic studies, e.g. microarray and proteomics studies. _____ can be found at http:// _____ .niaid.nih.gov or http:// _____ .abcc.ncifcrf.gov

Exam Probability: **Medium**

39. *Answer choices:*

(see index for correct answer)

- a. MolIDE
- b. DAVID
- c. FASTA
- d. PupaSuite

Guidance: level 1

:: Programming language implementation ::

In computing, a _____ is an emulation of a computer system. _____ s are based on computer architectures and provide functionality of a physical computer. Their implementations may involve specialized hardware, software, or a combination.

Exam Probability: **Low**

40. *Answer choices:*

(see index for correct answer)

- a. Man or boy test
- b. Funarg problem
- c. Protected mode
- d. Virtual machine

Guidance: level 1

:: Central processing unit ::

In computing, a _____ or array processor is a central processing unit that implements an instruction set containing instructions that operate on one-dimensional arrays of data called vectors, compared to the scalar processors, whose instructions operate on single data items. _____ s can greatly improve performance on certain workloads, notably numerical simulation and similar tasks. Vector machines appeared in the early 1970s and dominated supercomputer design through the 1970s into the 1990s, notably the various Cray platforms. The rapid fall in the price-to-performance ratio of conventional microprocessor designs led to the vector supercomputer`s demise in the later 1990s.

Exam Probability: **High**

41. *Answer choices:*

(see index for correct answer)

- a. Hardware register

- b. Vector processor
- c. Program status word
- d. Floating-point unit

Guidance: level 1

:: History of the Internet ::

_____ is a method of grouping data that is transmitted over a digital network into packets. Packets are made of a header and a payload. Data in the header are used by networking hardware to direct the packet to its destination where the payload is extracted and used by application software. _____ is the primary basis for data communications in computer networks worldwide.

Exam Probability: **Medium**

42. *Answer choices:*

(see index for correct answer)

- a. ALOHAnet
- b. Dot-com bubble
- c. ConnNet
- d. Packet switching

Guidance: level 1

:: Radio modulation modes ::

In telecommunications and signal processing, _____ is the encoding of information in a carrier wave by varying the instantaneous frequency of the wave.

Exam Probability: **High**

43. *Answer choices:*

(see index for correct answer)

- a. Quadrature amplitude modulation
- b. Frequency modulation
- c. Amplitude modulation
- d. Reduced-carrier transmission

Guidance: level 1

:: Digital electronics ::

_____ is a digital electronic data storage device, often used as computer memory, implemented with semiconductor electronic devices on an integrated circuit . There are many different types of implementations using various technologies.

Exam Probability: **Low**

44. *Answer choices:*

(see index for correct answer)

- a. LiquidHD
- b. Semiconductor memory
- c. Double data rate
- d. Logic redundancy

Guidance: level 1

:: Digital television ::

In signal processing, _____ , source coding, or bit-rate reduction involves encoding information using fewer bits than the original representation. Compression can be either lossy or lossless. Lossless compression reduces bits by identifying and eliminating statistical redundancy. No information is lost in lossless compression. Lossy compression reduces bits by removing unnecessary or less important information.

Exam Probability: **Medium**

45. *Answer choices:*

(see index for correct answer)

- a. Open IPTV
- b. Data compression
- c. Time slicing
- d. Video quality

:: Interrupts ::

In computer systems programming, an _____ , also known as an interrupt service routine or ISR, is a special block of code associated with a specific interrupt condition. _____ s are initiated by hardware interrupts, software interrupt instructions, or software exceptions, and are used for implementing device drivers or transitions between protected modes of operation, such as system calls.

Exam Probability: **Medium**

46. *Answer choices:*

(see index for correct answer)

- a. Interrupt handler
- b. End of interrupt
- c. INT 10H
- d. Interrupt vector

:: Internet architecture ::

_____ is defined as that aspect of Internet network engineering dealing with the issue of performance evaluation and performance optimization of operational IP networks. Traffic engineering encompasses the application of technology and scientific principles to the measurement, characterization, modeling, and control of Internet traffic [RFC-2702, AWD2].

Exam Probability: **Low**

47. *Answer choices:*

(see index for correct answer)

- a. Internet traffic engineering
- b. Internet bottleneck
- c. OpenURL knowledge base
- d. Multihoming

Guidance: level 1

:: Malware ::

The _____ is a story from the Trojan War about the subterfuge that the Greeks used to enter the independent city of Troy and win the war. In the canonical version, after a fruitless 10-year siege, the Greeks constructed a huge wooden horse, and hid a select force of men inside including Odysseus. The Greeks pretended to sail away, and the Trojans pulled the horse into their city as a victory trophy. That night the Greek force crept out of the horse and opened the gates for the rest of the Greek army, which had sailed back under cover of night. The Greeks entered and destroyed the city of Troy, ending the war.

48. *Answer choices:*

(see index for correct answer)

- a. Watering Hole
- b. Network Crack Program Hacker Group
- c. Power virus
- d. Dialer

Guidance: level 1

:: Network architecture ::

An _____ is a type of optical telecommunications network employing wired fiber-optic communication or wireless free-space optical communication in a mesh network architecture.

Exam Probability: **Medium**

49. *Answer choices:*

(see index for correct answer)

- a. Point of delivery
- b. Primary channel
- c. InterSwitch Trunk
- d. Optical mesh network

:: Device drivers ::

In computing, a _____ is a computer program that operates or controls a particular type of device that is attached to a computer. A driver provides a software interface to hardware devices, enabling operating systems and other computer programs to access hardware functions without needing to know precise details about the hardware being used.

Exam Probability: **High**

50. *Answer choices:*

(see index for correct answer)

- a. AMD Catalyst
- b. Mode setting
- c. Device driver
- d. Omega Drivers

:: History of the Internet ::

Electronic mail is a method of exchanging messages between people using electronic devices. Invented by Ray Tomlinson, _____ first entered limited use in the 1960s and by the mid-1970s had taken the form now recognized as _____ . _____ operates across computer networks, which today is primarily the Internet. Some early _____ systems required the author and the recipient to both be online at the same time, in common with instant messaging. Today's _____ systems are based on a store-and-forward model. _____ servers accept, forward, deliver, and store messages. Neither the users nor their computers are required to be online simultaneously; they need to connect only briefly, typically to a mail server or a webmail interface for as long as it takes to send or receive messages.

Exam Probability: **Low**

51. *Answer choices:*

(see index for correct answer)

- a. PicoSpan
- b. The Internet Hunt
- c. ConnNet
- d. MIDnet

Guidance: level 1

:: Computer storage devices ::

_____ , officially abbreviated as SD, is a non-volatile memory card format developed by the SD Card Association for use in portable devices.

52. *Answer choices:*

(see index for correct answer)

- a. Sun Open Storage
- b. BlackDog
- c. Secure Digital
- d. Nintendo DS storage devices

Guidance: level 1

:: Computer benchmarks ::

In computing, floating point operations per second is a measure of computer performance, useful in fields of scientific computations that require floating-point calculations. For such cases it is a more accurate measure than measuring instructions per second.

Exam Probability: **Low**

53. *Answer choices:*

(see index for correct answer)

- a. Server Efficiency Rating Tool
- b. FLOPS
- c. VMmark

- d. 3DMark

Guidance: level 1

:: Computer memory ::

In computing, a _____ is a reference to a specific memory location used at various levels by software and hardware. _____ es are fixed-length sequences of digits conventionally displayed and manipulated as unsigned integers. Such numerical semantic bases itself upon features of CPU , as well upon use of the memory like an array endorsed by various programming languages.

Exam Probability: **Low**

54. *Answer choices:*

(see index for correct answer)

- a. Content Addressable Parallel Processor
- b. EOS memory
- c. U61000
- d. Memory address

Guidance: level 1

:: Computer buses ::

In computing, the _____ , expansion board, adapter card or accessory card is a printed circuit board that can be inserted into an electrical connector, or expansion slot, on a computer motherboard, backplane or riser card to add functionality to a computer system via the expansion bus.

Exam Probability: **Medium**

55. *Answer choices:*

(see index for correct answer)

- a. Camera Link
- b. Peripheral bus
- c. PCI bus
- d. Expansion card

Guidance: level 1

:: Cache coherency ::

In computer architecture, _____ is the uniformity of shared resource data that ends up stored in multiple local caches. When clients in a system maintain caches of a common memory resource, problems may arise with incoherent data, which is particularly the case with CPUs in a multiprocessing system.

Exam Probability: **Medium**

56. *Answer choices:*

(see index for correct answer)

- a. MERSI protocol
- b. MOSI protocol
- c. MSI protocol
- d. Write-once

Guidance: level 1

:: Software architecture ::

The _____ is a form of user interface that allows users to interact with electronic devices through graphical icons and visual indicators such as secondary notation, instead of text-based user interfaces, typed command labels or text navigation. GUIs were introduced in reaction to the perceived steep learning curve of command-line interfaces , which require commands to be typed on a computer keyboard.

Exam Probability: **High**

57. *Answer choices:*

(see index for correct answer)

- a. Sun Web Developer Pack
- b. Situational application
- c. Domain-driven design
- d. Graphical user interface

:: Virtual reality ::

The _____ is the global system of interconnected computer networks that use the _____ protocol suite to link devices worldwide. It is a network of networks that consists of private, public, academic, business, and government networks of local to global scope, linked by a broad array of electronic, wireless, and optical networking technologies. The _____ carries a vast range of information resources and services, such as the inter-linked hypertext documents and applications of the World Wide Web , electronic mail, telephony, and file sharing.

Exam Probability: **Low**

58. *Answer choices:*

(see index for correct answer)

- a. Tony Parisi
- b. Draw distance
- c. Wirth Research
- d. Polynomial texture mapping

:: Classes of computers ::

_____ is the use of two or more central processing units within a single computer system. The term also refers to the ability of a system to support more than one processor or the ability to allocate tasks between them. There are many variations on this basic theme, and the definition of _____ can vary with context, mostly as a function of how CPUs are defined .

Exam Probability: **Low**

59. *Answer choices:*

(see index for correct answer)

- a. Plug compatible
- b. Laptop
- c. Locale
- d. Multiprocessing

Guidance: level 1

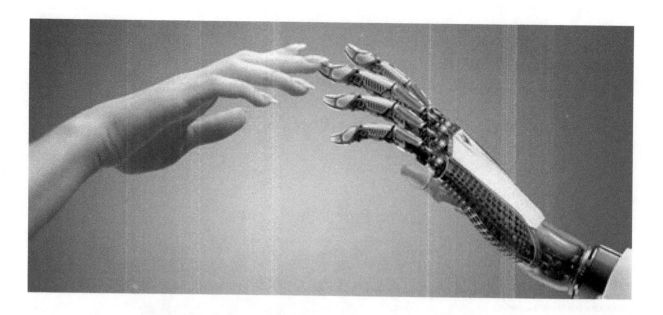

Human-computer interaction

Human–computer interaction researches the design and use of computer technology, focused on the interfaces between people (users) and computers. Researchers in the field of HCI both observe the ways in which humans interact with computers and design technologies that let humans interact with computers in novel ways. As a field of research, human–computer interaction is situated at the intersection of computer science, behavioral sciences, design, media studies, and several other fields of study.

:: Data serialization formats ::

In computing, _____ s, sexprs or sexps are a notation for nested list data, invented for and popularized by the programming language Lisp, which uses them for source code as well as data. In the usual parenthesized syntax of Lisp, an _____ is classically defined as

Exam Probability: **High**

1. *Answer choices:*

(see index for correct answer)

- a. Tab-separated values
- b. Simple Object Access Protocol
- c. Action Message Format
- d. S-expression

Guidance: level 1

:: World Wide Web ::

_____ is an attack on a website that changes the visual appearance of a website or a web page. These are typically the work of defacers, who break into a web server and replace the hosted website with one of their own. Defacement is generally meant as a kind of electronic graffiti and, as other forms of vandalism, is also used to spread messages by politically motivated "cyber protesters" or hacktivists. Methods such as a web shell may be used to aid in _____ .

Exam Probability: **High**

2. *Answer choices:*

(see index for correct answer)

- a. Sticky content
- b. Web property
- c. Webvet

- d. Website defacement

Guidance: level 1

:: Software design ::

Design can refer to such a plan or specification or to the created object, etc., and features of it such as aesthetic, functional, economic or socio-political.

Exam Probability: **High**

3. *Answer choices:*
(see index for correct answer)

- a. Decomposition
- b. Design rationale
- c. Oslo
- d. Systems design

Guidance: level 1

:: Usability ::

_____ is the ease of use and learnability of a human-made object such as a tool or device. In software engineering, _____ is the degree to which a software can be used by specified consumers to achieve quantified objectives with effectiveness, efficiency, and satisfaction in a quantified context of use.

Exam Probability: **Low**

4. *Answer choices:*

(see index for correct answer)

- a. Universal usability
- b. Jared Spool
- c. Card sorting
- d. Project Oxygen

Guidance: level 1

:: Computing input devices ::

A _____ is a computer that interacts with the user through the surface of an ordinary object, rather than through a monitor, keyboard, mouse, or other physical hardware.

Exam Probability: **Medium**

5. *Answer choices:*

- a. Project Digits
- b. Surface computer
- c. Mir:ror
- d. Orbita mouse

Guidance: level 1

:: Usability ::

_____ or user interface engineering is the design of user interfaces for machines and software, such as computers, home appliances, mobile devices, and other electronic devices, with the focus on maximizing usability and the user experience. The goal of _____ is to make the user's interaction as simple and efficient as possible, in terms of accomplishing user goals .

Exam Probability: **Medium**

6. *Answer choices:*

- a. Card sorting
- b. System utility
- c. DWIM
- d. Bodystorming

:: User interfaces ::

The _____ , in the industrial design field of human–computer interaction, is the space where interactions between humans and machines occur. The goal of this interaction is to allow effective operation and control of the machine from the human end, whilst the machine simultaneously feeds back information that aids the operators' decision-making process. Examples of this broad concept of _____ s include the interactive aspects of computer operating systems, hand tools, heavy machinery operator controls, and process controls. The design considerations applicable when creating _____ s are related to or involve such disciplines as ergonomics and psychology.

Exam Probability: **Medium**

7. *Answer choices:*

(see index for correct answer)

- a. Light-on-dark color scheme
- b. User interface
- c. Froxlor
- d. Flight envelope protection

:: User interfaces ::

A _____ is a graphical control element which poses an information area typically found at the window's bottom. It can be divided into sections to group information. Its job is primarily to display information about the current state of its window, although some _____ s have extra functionality. For example, many web browsers have clickable sections that pop up a display of security or privacy information.

Exam Probability: **Low**

8. *Answer choices:*

(see index for correct answer)

- a. Natural language user interface
- b. Video wall
- c. Light-on-dark color scheme
- d. Desktop metaphor

Guidance: level 1

:: Computing input devices ::

A _____ is an electronic device which attempts to convert the motions of a sign language into written or spoken words. The potential of such gloves to do this is commonly overstated or totally misunderstood, because sign languages have a complex grammar that includes use of the sign space and facial expressions .

Exam Probability: **Medium**

9. *Answer choices:*

(see index for correct answer)

- a. Ofoto
- b. Sign language glove
- c. FaceVsion
- d. Samples per inch

Guidance: level 1

:: Speech recognition ::

The _____ is a highly efficient C++ library that handles finite state machines; in particular it deals with weighted and unweighted automata and transducers. It has been designed to be used in a variety of natural language processing applications and was tested with speech recognition and machine translation. It is available under an open-source license.

Exam Probability: **Low**

10. *Answer choices:*

(see index for correct answer)

- a. RWTH FSA Toolkit
- b. Speech acquisition
- c. Transcription
- d. Trigram

:: Multimodal interaction ::

_____ is the term for computer generated tactile sensations over a network, between physically distant human beings, or between a local user and a remote location, using sensors and effectors. Microcontrollers input information from sensors, and control effectors to create human sensations as outputs.

Exam Probability: **Medium**

11. *Answer choices:*

(see index for correct answer)

- a. Computer-supported cooperative work
- b. Modality
- c. Interactive media
- d. EyeTap

:: User interfaces ::

_____ is a specialised visual software localization tool developed to enable the translation of user interfaces.

Exam Probability: **Medium**

12. *Answer choices:*

(see index for correct answer)

- a. The Humane Interface
- b. SDL Passolo
- c. Laster Technologies
- d. Scratch input

Guidance: level 1

:: World Wide Web ::

In digital marketing and online advertising, _____ is the deliberate manipulation of search engine indexes. It involves a number of methods, such as link building and repeating unrelated phrases, to manipulate the relevance or prominence of resources indexed, in a manner inconsistent with the purpose of the indexing system.

Exam Probability: **Low**

13. *Answer choices:*

(see index for correct answer)

- a. Spamdexing
- b. Change detection and notification
- c. Open Market For Internet Content Accessibility
- d. ChuvashTet

Guidance: level 1

:: Virtual reality ::

The _____ is a removable device from Nintendo which provides force feedback while playing video games. Games that support the _____ cause it to vibrate in select situations, such as when firing a weapon or receiving damage, to immerse the player in the game. Versions of the _____ are available for the Nintendo 64, the Nintendo DS, and the Nintendo DS Lite. A select few Game Boy Color and Game Boy Advance games use a similar technology built into the game cartridge. Force feedback vibration has become a built-in standard feature in almost every home video game console controller since.

Exam Probability: **Medium**

14. *Answer choices:*

(see index for correct answer)

- a. Rumble Pak
- b. Stroker Serpentine
- c. Campustours
- d. 3DML

:: Voice technology ::

Voice stress analysis and computer voice stress analysis are collectively a pseudoscientific technology that aims to infer deception from stress measured in the voice. The CVSA records the human voice using a microphone, and the technology is based on the tenet that the non-verbal, low-frequency content of the voice conveys information about the physiological and psychological state of the speaker. Typically utilized in investigative settings, the technology aims to differentiate between stressed and non-stressed outputs in response to stimuli , with high stress seen as an indication of deception.

Exam Probability: **High**

15. *Answer choices:*

(see index for correct answer)

- a. Microsoft Speech Server
- b. Electroglottographic wavegram
- c. Lessac Technologies
- d. Voice analysis

:: Computer keyboards ::

A _____ is a type of vehicle crash in which a vehicle tips over onto its side or roof. _____ s have a higher fatality rate than other types of vehicle collisions.

Exam Probability: **Low**

16. *Answer choices:*

(see index for correct answer)

- a. Scancode
- b. Logitech G19
- c. Rollover
- d. Photovoltaic keyboard

Guidance: level 1

:: Webcams ::

The _____ is a color digital camera device, similar to a webcam, for the PlayStation 2. The technology uses computer vision and gesture recognition to process images taken by the camera. This allows players to interact with games using motion, color detection, and also sound, through its built-in microphone. It was released in October 2003.

Exam Probability: **Low**

17. *Answer choices:*

(see index for correct answer)

- a. EyeToy
- b. Cheese
- c. Ubisoft Motion Tracking Camera
- d. Western Wall camera

Guidance: level 1

:: Computing input devices ::

A _____ is an input interface that allows a user to input spatial data to a computer. CAD systems and graphical user interfaces allow the user to control and provide data to the computer using physical gestures by moving a hand-held mouse or similar device across the surface of the physical desktop and activating switches on the mouse. Movements of the _____ are echoed on the screen by movements of the pointer and other visual changes. Common gestures are point and click and drag and drop.

Exam Probability: **Medium**

18. *Answer choices:*

(see index for correct answer)

- a. Anoto
- b. Mimio
- c. Mouse keys
- d. Kinect

:: Usability ::

_____ is the inclusive practice of ensuring there are no barriers that prevent interaction with, or access to, websites on the World Wide Web by people with disabilities. When sites are correctly designed, developed and edited, generally all users have equal access to information and functionality.

Exam Probability: **Low**

19. *Answer choices:*

(see index for correct answer)

- a. Web accessibility
- b. Heat map
- c. RITE Method
- d. Questionnaire for User Interaction Satisfaction

:: Debuggers ::

_____ is the process of finding and resolving defects or problems within a computer program that prevent correct operation of computer software or a system.

Exam Probability: **High**

20. *Answer choices:*

(see index for correct answer)

- a. CodeView
- b. Jasik debugger
- c. Microsoft Visual Studio Debugger
- d. Advanced Debugger

Guidance: level 1

:: World Wide Web ::

The _____ is a W3C Recommendation. RIF is part of the infrastructure for the semantic web, along with SPARQL, RDF and OWL. Although originally envisioned by many as a "rules layer" for the semantic web, in reality the design of RIF is based on the observation that there are many "rules languages" in existence, and what is needed is to exchange rules between them.

Exam Probability: **Low**

21. *Answer choices:*

(see index for correct answer)

- a. Swagbucks
- b. Augmented browsing
- c. Rule Interchange Format
- d. Socialcasting

Guidance: level 1

:: Virtual reality ::

An _____ , a concept in Hinduism that means "descent", refers to the material appearance or incarnation of a deity on earth. The relative verb to "alight, to make one's appearance" is sometimes used to refer to any guru or revered human being.

Exam Probability: **Low**

22. *Answer choices:*

(see index for correct answer)

- a. Avatar
- b. Environmental Audio Extensions
- c. Eve Online
- d. Sculpted prim

Guidance: level 1

:: Control characters ::

_____ is the boundless three-dimensional extent in which objects and events have relative position and direction. Physical _____ is often conceived in three linear dimensions, although modern physicists usually consider it, with time, to be part of a boundless four-dimensional continuum known as _____ time. The concept of _____ is considered to be of fundamental importance to an understanding of the physical universe. However, disagreement continues between philosophers over whether it is itself an entity, a relationship between entities, or part of a conceptual framework.

Exam Probability: **Medium**

23. *Answer choices:*

(see index for correct answer)

- a. Space
- b. Hard space
- c. Control character
- d. Bell character

Guidance: level 1

:: Speech recognition ::

_____ is the process of analyzing recorded calls to gather customer information to improve communication and future interaction. The process is primarily used by customer contact centers to extract information buried in client interactions with an enterprise. Although _____ includes elements of automatic speech recognition, it is known for analyzing the topic being discussed, which is weighed against the emotional character of the speech and the amount and locations of speech versus non-speech during the interaction. _____ in contact centers can be used to mine recorded customer interactions to surface the intelligence essential for building effective cost containment and customer service strategies. The technology can pinpoint cost drivers, trend analysis, identify strengths and weaknesses with processes and products, and help understand how the marketplace perceives offerings.

Exam Probability: **High**

24. *Answer choices:*

(see index for correct answer)

- a. Time-inhomogeneous hidden Bernoulli model
- b. Subvocal recognition
- c. N-gram
- d. Speech analytics

Guidance: level 1

:: Human-based computation ::

_____ is "an activity through which collective human actions organize knowledge." It is the creation and processing of information by a group of people. As an academic field _____ studies the information processing power of networked social systems.

Exam Probability: **Low**

25. *Answer choices:*

(see index for correct answer)

- a. Social information processing
- b. Crowdreferencing
- c. Ubiquitous human computing
- d. Human-based computation

Guidance: level 1

:: Usability ::

_____ website. Some broad goals of usability are the presentation of information and choices in a clear and concise way, a lack of ambiguity and the placement of important items in appropriate areas. Another important element of _____ is ensuring that the content works on various devices and browsers.

Exam Probability: **High**

26. *Answer choices:*

(see index for correct answer)

- a. Web usability
- b. Scenario
- c. Usability engineering
- d. Jared Spool

Guidance: level 1

:: User interfaces ::

_____ is the practice of presenting information in a way that fosters efficient and effective understanding of it. The term has come to be used specifically for graphic design for displaying information effectively, rather than just attractively or for artistic expression. _____ is closely related to the field of data visualization and is often taught as part of graphic design courses.

Exam Probability: **Medium**

27. *Answer choices:*
(see index for correct answer)

- a. Information design
- b. System console
- c. Baifox
- d. Operating environment

:: History of computing ::

In "As We May Think", Bush describes a _____ as an electromechanical device enabling individuals to develop and read a large self-contained research library, create and follow associative trails of links and personal annotations, and recall these trails at any time to share them with other researchers. This device would closely mimic the associative processes of the human mind, but it would be gifted with permanent recollection. As Bush writes, "Thus science may implement the ways in which man produces, stores, and consults the record of the race".

Exam Probability: **High**

28. *Answer choices:*

(see index for correct answer)

- a. C.mmp
- b. Charles Babbage Institute
- c. Plan calcul
- d. Strategic Computing Initiative

:: Automatic identification and data capture ::

_____ , also called Smart Tag, is an extremely flat configured transponder under a conventional print-coded label, which includes chip, antenna and bonding wires as a so-called inlay. The labels, made of paper, fabric or plastics, are prepared as a paper roll with the inlays laminated between the rolled carrier and the label media for use in specially-designed printer units.

Exam Probability: **Medium**

29. *Answer choices:*

(see index for correct answer)

- a. Automatic number plate recognition
- b. HipVoice
- c. Smart label
- d. Magnetic ink character recognition

Guidance: level 1

:: Usability ::

In systems engineering, the _____ is a simple, ten-item attitude Likert scale giving a global view of subjective assessments of usability. It was developed by John Brooke at Digital Equipment Corporation in the UK in 1986 as a tool to be used in usability engineering of electronic office systems.

Exam Probability: **Low**

30. *Answer choices:*

(see index for correct answer)

- a. InstaLoad
- b. Usability testing
- c. Process-centered design
- d. System Usability Scale

Guidance: level 1

:: Database management systems ::

_____ s or data _____ s are computer languages used to make queries in databases and information systems.

Exam Probability: **Medium**

31. *Answer choices:*

(see index for correct answer)

- a. Object-based spatial database
- b. SciDB
- c. Query language
- d. Database engine

Guidance: level 1

:: World Wide Web ::

The _____ is the W3C recommended method for describing Web resources. It specifies a protocol for publishing metadata about Web resources using RDF, OWL, and HTTP.

Exam Probability: **Medium**

32. *Answer choices:*

(see index for correct answer)

- a. Noindex
- b. Automated online assistant
- c. Smart-M3
- d. Isabel Maxwell

Guidance: level 1

:: Virtual reality ::

A _____ is a three-dimensional software model or representation of the Earth or another world. A _____ provides the user with the ability to freely move around in the virtual environment by changing the viewing angle and position. Compared to a conventional globe, _____ s have the additional capability of representing many different views on the surface of the Earth. These views may be of geographical features, man-made features such as roads and buildings, or abstract representations of demographic quantities such as population.

Exam Probability: **High**

33. *Answer choices:*

(see index for correct answer)

- a. Ancient Qumran: A Virtual Reality Tour
- b. Perpetuum
- c. Virtual globe
- d. Ty Girlz

Guidance: level 1

:: Human-based computation ::

_____ is a CAPTCHA-like system designed to establish that a computer user is human and, at the same time, assist in the digitization of books. _____ was originally developed by Luis von Ahn, David Abraham, Manuel Blum, Michael Crawford, Ben Maurer, Colin McMillen, and Edison Tan at Carnegie Mellon University's main Pittsburgh campus. It was acquired by Google in September 2009.

34. *Answer choices:*

(see index for correct answer)

- a. Galaxy Zoo
- b. ReCAPTCHA
- c. Human-based computation game
- d. Txtm8

Guidance: level 1

:: Free windowing systems ::

_____ is a 2.5D desktop environment. More specifically, it is a X window manager with many features that set it apart from the traditional 3D "cube" workspace. Windows can be turned 3 dimensionally in any direction, enabling the user to fit more windows onto a screen, and they can be scaled, all while remaining fully operational. The development team has avoided such effects as wobbly windows, giving functionality and productivity higher priority than eye candy.

Exam Probability: **Low**

35. *Answer choices:*

(see index for correct answer)

- a. Rio

- b. Mir
- c. XFree86
- d. Metisse

Guidance: level 1

:: Virtual reality ::

In 3D computer graphics, _____ , or Dot3 bump mapping, is a technique used for faking the lighting of bumps and dents – an implementation of bump mapping. It is used to add details without using more polygons. A common use of this technique is to greatly enhance the appearance and details of a low polygon model by generating a normal map from a high polygon model or height map.

Exam Probability: **High**

36. *Answer choices:*

(see index for correct answer)

- a. 3D user interaction
- b. Eve Online
- c. Normal mapping
- d. Id Tech 4

Guidance: level 1

:: Computing input devices ::

A _____ is a type of image scanner for making scans of rare books and other easily damaged documents. In essence, such a scanner is a mounted camera taking photos of a well-lit environment. Originally, such scanners were expensive and could only be found in archives and museums, but with the availability of cheap, high-resolution digital cameras, DIY _____ s have become affordable, and for instance are being used by volunteer scan providers for Project Gutenberg.

Exam Probability: **High**

37. *Answer choices:*

(see index for correct answer)

- a. Mousepad
- b. Trackball
- c. Planetary scanner
- d. Duplex scanning

Guidance: level 1

:: Virtual reality ::

_____ is defined as integrating geometric models and related engineering tools such as analysis, simulation, optimization, and decision making tools, etc., within a computer-generated environment that facilitates multidisciplinary collaborative product development. _____ shares many characteristics with software engineering, such as the ability to obtain many different results through different implementations.

Exam Probability: **Low**

38. *Answer choices:*
(see index for correct answer)

- a. Stroker Serpentine
- b. Virtual engineering
- c. Campustours
- d. Avizo

Guidance: level 1

:: Ergonomics ::

A _____ uses the same principles in its design as an equestrian saddle. It is equipped with a chair base on casters and a gas cylinder for adjusting the correct sitting height. The casters enable moving around and reaching out for objects while sitting. Some _____ s have backrests, but most do not.

Exam Probability: **High**

39. *Answer choices:*

(see index for correct answer)

- a. Computer-aided ergonomics
- b. ToggleKeys
- c. Principle of least astonishment
- d. Light ergonomics

Guidance: level 1

:: Graphical user interface elements ::

In computer interface design, a _____ is a graphical control element on which on-screen buttons, icons, menus, or other input or output elements are placed. _____ s are seen in many types of software such as office suites, graphics editors and web browsers. _____ s are usually distinguished from palettes by their integration into the edges of the screen or larger windows, which results in wasted space if too many underpopulated bars are stacked atop each other or interface inefficiency if overloaded bars are placed on small windows.

Exam Probability: **High**

40. *Answer choices:*

(see index for correct answer)

- a. Context menu
- b. Shelf

- c. modal dialog
- d. Toolbar

Guidance: level 1

:: Speech recognition ::

_____ is a speech recognition component developed by Microsoft for the Windows Vista operating system that enables the use of voice commands to control the desktop user interface; dictate text in electronic documents and email; navigate websites; perform keyboard shortcuts; and to operate the mouse cursor. It also supports the creation of custom macros to perform additional tasks.

Exam Probability: **Medium**

41. *Answer choices:*

(see index for correct answer)

- a. Non-native speech database
- b. Voice activity detection
- c. Windows Speech Recognition
- d. HTK

Guidance: level 1

:: World Wide Web ::

_____ is a concept, that proposes that the World Wide Web has, or could, evolve into an entity worthy of consideration as a life form in its own right; a new posthuman species consisting of just one isolated member.

Exam Probability: **High**

42. *Answer choices:*

(see index for correct answer)

- a. Web life
- b. DBpedia
- c. Open Web
- d. Noindex

Guidance: level 1

:: Ubiquitous computing ::

_____ is a concept in software engineering and computer science where computing is made to appear anytime and everywhere. In contrast to desktop computing, _____ can occur using any device, in any location, and in any format. A user interacts with the computer, which can exist in many different forms, including laptop computers, tablets and terminals in everyday objects such as a refrigerator or a pair of glasses. The underlying technologies to support _____ include Internet, advanced middleware, operating system, mobile code, sensors, microprocessors, new I/O and user interfaces, networks, mobile protocols, location and positioning, and new materials.

43. *Answer choices:*

(see index for correct answer)

- a. Wireless lock
- b. ZOMM
- c. Personal and Ubiquitous Computing
- d. Ubiquitous computing

Guidance: level 1

:: Virtual reality ::

A _____ is an overlay of augmented sensory information upon a user's perception of a real environment in order to improve human performance in both direct and remotely manipulated tasks. Developed in the early 1990s by Louis Rosenberg at the U.S. Air Force Research Laboratory, _____ s was a pioneering platform in virtual reality and augmented reality technologies.

Exam Probability: **Low**

44. *Answer choices:*

(see index for correct answer)

- a. Virtuality
- b. Virtual acoustic space

- c. Virtual fixture
- d. Next Limit Technologies

Guidance: level 1

:: Virtual reality ::

The _____ is a proposed, in development virtual reality helmet that will allegedly stimulate all five of the human senses when it is finished.

Exam Probability: **High**

45. *Answer choices:*

(see index for correct answer)

- a. Virtual Cocoon
- b. Wirth Research
- c. Eon Reality
- d. Next Limit Technologies

Guidance: level 1

:: Multimodal interaction ::

_____ is a book series by Myron W. Krueger about interactive immersive environments , based on video recognition techniques, that put a user in full, unencumbered contact with the digital world. He started this work in the late 1960s and is considered to be a key figure in the early innovation of virtual reality. _____ was published in 1983 and updated in _____ II in 1991 .

Exam Probability: **Low**

46. *Answer choices:*

(see index for correct answer)

- a. Collaborative working environment
- b. Artificial reality
- c. Mixed reality
- d. International Community for Auditory Display

Guidance: level 1

:: Photo software ::

_____ is a raster graphics editor developed and published by Adobe Inc. for Windows and macOS. It was originally created in 1988 by Thomas and John Knoll. Since then, this software has become the industry standard not only in raster graphics editing, but in digital art as a whole. The software's name has thus become a generic trademark, leading to its usage as a verb although Adobe discourages such use. Photoshop can edit and compose raster images in multiple layers and supports masks, alpha compositing, and several color models including RGB, CMYK, CIELAB, spot color, and duotone. Photoshop uses its own <code>PSD</code> and <code>PSB</code> file formats to support these features. In addition to raster graphics, this software has limited abilities to edit or render text and vector graphics , as well as 3D graphics and video. Its feature set can be expanded by plug-ins; programs developed and distributed independently of Photoshop that run inside it and offer new or enhanced features.

Exam Probability: **Low**

47. *Answer choices:*

(see index for correct answer)

- a. Fotoflexer
- b. Adobe Photoshop
- c. Word Lens
- d. ViewMinder

Guidance: level 1

:: Virtual reality ::

_____ , is a Space Shuttle stand-alone mission simulator for Microsoft Windows. The simulator was released on January 1, 2008 after having been under development for more than six years.

Exam Probability: **High**

48. *Answer choices:*

(see index for correct answer)

- a. Space Shuttle Mission 2007
- b. Virtual reality cue reactivity
- c. Vortex
- d. Mscape

Guidance: level 1

:: Virtual reality ::

A _____ is a computer-based simulated environment which may be populated by many users who can create a personal avatar, and simultaneously and independently explore the _____ , participate in its activities and communicate with others. These avatars can be textual, two or three-dimensional graphical representations, or live video avatars with auditory and touch sensations. In general, _____ s allow for multiple users but single player computer games, such as Skyrim, can also be considered a type of _____ .

Exam Probability: **Low**

49. *Answer choices:*

- a. Graphics Turing Test
- b. Next Limit Technologies
- c. Amira
- d. Virtual world

Guidance: level 1

:: World Wide Web ::

_____ is the effort by taxonomists to use the World Wide Web in order to create unified, consensus taxonomies of life on Earth.

Exam Probability: **Medium**

50. *Answer choices:*

- a. Web Single Sign-On Metadata Exchange Protocol
- b. Automated online assistant
- c. Web-based taxonomy
- d. Party of Internet Democracy

Guidance: level 1

:: Computer keyboards ::

A _____ is a software component that allows the input of characters without the need for physical keys. The interaction with the _____ happens mostly via a touchscreen interface, but can also take place in a different form in virtual or augmented reality.

Exam Probability: **High**

51. *Answer choices:*

(see index for correct answer)

- a. Alt code
- b. Thumb keyboard
- c. Virtual keyboard
- d. Keyboard matrix circuit

Guidance: level 1

:: Computing input devices ::

A _____ is a kind of television tuner that allows television signals to be received by a computer. Most TV tuners also function as video capture cards, allowing them to record television programs onto a hard disk much like the digital video recorder does.

52. *Answer choices:*

(see index for correct answer)

- a. TV tuner card
- b. Planetary scanner
- c. CrossPad
- d. Film scanner

Guidance: level 1

:: Hypertext ::

_____ is text displayed on a computer display or other electronic devices with references to other text that the reader can immediately access. _____ documents are interconnected by hyperlinks, which are typically activated by a mouse click, keypress set or by touching the screen. Apart from text, the term " _____ " is also sometimes used to describe tables, images, and other presentational content formats with integrated hyperlinks. _____ is one of the key underlying concepts of the World Wide Web, where Web pages are often written in the _____ Markup Language . As implemented on the Web, _____ enables the easy-to-use publication of information over the Internet.

53. *Answer choices:*

(see index for correct answer)

- a. Hyperlink
- b. Elfland catacombs
- c. Internal link
- d. Hypertext

Guidance: level 1

:: GUI widgets ::

A _____ or option button is a graphical control element that allows the user to choose only one of a predefined set of mutually exclusive options. The singular property of a _____ makes it distinct from a checkbox, which allows more than one item to be selected and for the unselected state to be restored.

Exam Probability: **High**

54. *Answer choices:*

(see index for correct answer)

- a. Slider
- b. Ribbon
- c. Combo box
- d. Radio button

Guidance: level 1

:: Human–computer interaction ::

A _____ is a small, but demographically diverse group of people and whose reactions are studied especially in market research or political analysis in guided or open discussions about a new product or something else to determine the reactions that can be expected from a larger population. It is a form of qualitative research consisting of interviews in which a group of people are asked about their perceptions, opinions, beliefs, and attitudes towards a product, service, concept, advertisement, idea, or packaging. Questions are asked in an interactive group setting where participants are free to talk with other group members. During this process, the researcher either takes notes or records the vital points he or she is getting from the group. Researchers should select members of the _____ carefully for effective and authoritative responses.

Exam Probability: **Medium**

55. *Answer choices:*

(see index for correct answer)

- a. Thanatosensitivity
- b. Humanistic intelligence
- c. Focus group
- d. Human action cycle

Guidance: level 1

:: User interfaces ::

The _____ is a user interface design theory to measure the amount of attention that is required to perform certain tasks in a web application. It is developed by Antradar Software in an attempt to benchmark the ease of use of open source CMS products and to monitor the trend of UI designs.

Exam Probability: **Medium**

56. *Answer choices:*

(see index for correct answer)

- a. Intelligent user interface
- b. Preview
- c. Principles of attention stress
- d. State management

Guidance: level 1

:: Internet terminology ::

A _____ is a discussion or informational website published on the World Wide Web consisting of discrete, often informal diary-style text entries . Posts are typically displayed in reverse chronological order, so that the most recent post appears first, at the top of the web page. Until 2009, _____ s were usually the work of a single individual, occasionally of a small group, and often covered a single subject or topic. In the 2010s, "multi-author _____ s" emerged, featuring the writing of multiple authors and sometimes professionally edited. MABs from newspapers, other media outlets, universities, think tanks, advocacy groups, and similar institutions account for an increasing quantity of _____ traffic. The rise of Twitter and other "micro _____ ging" systems helps integrate MABs and single-author _____ s into the news media. _____ can also be used as a verb, meaning to maintain or add content to a _____ .

Exam Probability: **Low**

57. *Answer choices:*

(see index for correct answer)

- a. Hindi blogosphere
- b. Lettrs
- c. Snail mail
- d. Blog

Guidance: level 1

:: World Wide Web ::

A _____ is a type of website which provides a service for webmasters in exchange for traffic. It is similar to the autosurf concept with the exception that _____ s usually use a manual rotation.

Exam Probability: **High**

58. *Answer choices:*

(see index for correct answer)

- a. World Wide Web Foundation
- b. Instant WebKiosk
- c. Protocol for Web Description Resources
- d. Traffic exchange

Guidance: level 1

:: Speech recognition ::

The idea of surfing the web by voice dates back to at least the work of Hemphill and Thrift in 1995 who developed a system in which, HTML pages were downloaded and processed on client-side computers enabling voice access to web page content, and activation of hyperlinks through spoken commands.

Exam Probability: **Medium**

59. *Answer choices:*

(see index for correct answer)

- a. JSGF
- b. Audio mining
- c. SpeechWeb
- d. Speech acquisition

Guidance: level 1

Software engineering

Software engineering include is the systematic application of scientific and technological knowledge, methods, and experience to the design, implementation, testing, and documentation of software

---

:: Functional programming ::

In computer science, _____ is a programming paradigm—a style of building the structure and elements of computer programs—that treats computation as the evaluation of mathematical functions and avoids changing-state and mutable data. It is a declarative programming paradigm in that programming is done with expressions or declarations instead of statements. Functional code is idempotent: a function's return value depends only on its arguments, so calling a function with the same value for an argument always produces the same result. This is in contrast to imperative programming where, in addition to a function's arguments, global program state can affect a function's resulting value. Eliminating side effects, that is, changes in state that do not depend on the function inputs, can make understanding a program easier, which is one of the key motivations for the development of _____ .

Exam Probability: **Low**

1. *Answer choices:*

(see index for correct answer)

- a. mutable
- b. Functional programming

Guidance: level 1

:: Computer file systems ::

In computing, a _____ or filesystem controls how data is stored and retrieved. Without a _____ , information placed in a storage medium would be one large body of data with no way to tell where one piece of information stops and the next begins. By separating the data into pieces and giving each piece a name, the information is easily isolated and identified. Taking its name from the way paper-based information systems are named, each group of data is called a "file". The structure and logic rules used to manage the groups of information and their names is called a " _____ ".

Exam Probability: **High**

2. *Answer choices:*

(see index for correct answer)

- a. Installable File System
- b. Boot sector
- c. Hierarchical File System
- d. File system

Guidance: level 1

:: Debuggers ::

A _____ or debugging tool is a computer program that is used to test and debug other programs . The code to be examined might alternatively be running on an instruction set simulator , a technique that allows great power in its ability to halt when specific conditions are encountered, but which will typically be somewhat slower than executing the code directly on the appropriate processor. Some _____ s offer two modes of operation, full or partial simulation, to limit this impact.

Exam Probability: **High**

3. *Answer choices:*

(see index for correct answer)

- a. DTrace
- b. Nemiver
- c. KGDB
- d. KDbg

Guidance: level 1

:: Simulation programming languages ::

_____ is the name of two _____ tion programming languages, _____ I and _____ 67, developed in the 1960s at the Norwegian Computing Center in Oslo, by Ole-Johan Dahl and Kristen Nygaard. Syntactically, it is a fairly faithful superset of ALGOL 60, also influenced by the design of Simscript.

4. *Answer choices:*

(see index for correct answer)

- a. Stateflow
- b. SIMSCRIPT
- c. Modelica
- d. Simula

Guidance: level 1

:: Data types ::

In programming languages, a _____ is a set of rules that assigns a property called type to the various constructs of a computer program, such as variables, expressions, functions or modules. These types formalize and enforce the otherwise implicit categories the programmer uses for algebraic data types, data structures, or other components . The main purpose of a _____ is to reduce possibilities for bugs in computer programs by defining interfaces between different parts of a computer program, and then checking that the parts have been connected in a consistent way. This checking can happen statically , dynamically , or as a combination of static and dynamic checking. _____ s have other purposes as well, such as expressing business rules, enabling certain compiler optimizations, allowing for multiple dispatch, providing a form of documentation, etc.

5. *Answer choices:*

- a. Union type
- b. Handle
- c. Single-precision floating-point format
- d. Type system

Guidance: level 1

:: Data modeling languages ::

An _____ is a description of a type of XML document, typically expressed in terms of constraints on the structure and content of documents of that type, above and beyond the basic syntactical constraints imposed by XML itself. These constraints are generally expressed using some combination of grammatical rules governing the order of elements, Boolean predicates that the content must satisfy, data types governing the content of elements and attributes, and more specialized rules such as uniqueness and referential integrity constraints.

Exam Probability: **Low**

6. *Answer choices:*

- a. Binary Format Description language
- b. Soma File

- c. TimeML
- d. Data Format Description Language

Guidance: level 1

:: Data types ::

In computer science, an _____ is a mathematical model for data types, where a data type is defined by its behavior from the point of view of a user of the data, specifically in terms of possible values, possible operations on data of this type, and the behavior of these operations. This contrasts with data structures, which are concrete representations of data, and are the point of view of an implementer, not a user.

Exam Probability: **Medium**

7. *Answer choices:*

(see index for correct answer)

- a. Abstract data type
- b. Product type
- c. Run-time type information
- d. Bottom type

Guidance: level 1

:: Formal languages ::

A _____ is a mark, sign or word that indicates, signifies, or is understood as representing an idea, object, or relationship. _____ s allow people to go beyond what is known or seen by creating linkages between otherwise very different concepts and experiences. All communication is achieved through the use of _____ s. _____ s take the form of words, sounds, gestures, ideas or visual images and are used to convey other ideas and beliefs. For example, a red octagon may be a _____ for "STOP". On a map, a blue line might represent a river. Numerals are _____ s for numbers. Alphabetic letters may be _____ s for sounds. Personal names are _____ s representing individuals. A red rose may _____ ize love and compassion. The variable `x`, in a mathematical equation, may _____ ize the position of a particle in space.

Exam Probability: **Low**

8. *Answer choices:*

(see index for correct answer)

- a. Uniquely inversible grammar
- b. Symbol
- c. Weak generative capacity
- d. Finite thickness

Guidance: level 1

:: Data types ::

The _____ is a unit of digital information that most commonly consists of eight bits, representing a binary number. Historically, the _____ was the number of bits used to encode a single character of text in a computer and for this reason it is the smallest addressable unit of memory in many computer architectures.

Exam Probability: **High**

9. *Answer choices:*

(see index for correct answer)

- a. Boolean data type
- b. HRESULT
- c. Byte
- d. Polymorphism

Guidance: level 1

:: Cloud computing providers ::

_____ , Inc. was an American company that sold computers, computer components, software, and information technology services and created the Java programming language, the Solaris operating system, ZFS, the Network File System , and SPARC. Sun contributed significantly to the evolution of several key computing technologies, among them Unix, RISC processors, thin client computing, and virtualized computing. Sun was founded on February 24, 1982. At its height, the Sun headquarters were in Santa Clara, California , on the former west campus of the Agnews Developmental Center.

10. *Answer choices:*

(see index for correct answer)

- a. Ninefold
- b. Sun Microsystems
- c. NaviSite
- d. T-Systems

Guidance: level 1

:: Discourse analysis ::

_____ is a general-purpose document processor. It is especially suited for structured documents, automated document production, very fine typography, and multi-lingual typesetting. It is based in part on the TeX typesetting system, and uses a document markup language for manuscript preparation. The typographical and automated capabilities of _____ are extensive, including interfaces for handling microtypography, multiple footnotes and footnote classes, and manipulating OpenType fonts and features. Moreover, it offers extensive support for colors, backgrounds, hyperlinks, presentations, figure-text integration, and conditional compilation. It gives the user extensive control over formatting while making it easy to create new layouts and styles without learning the low-level TeX macro language.

11. *Answer choices:*

- a. Chantal Mouffe
- b. Open discourse
- c. Recontextualisation
- d. ConTeXt

Guidance: level 1

:: Software quality ::

Many aspects of structural quality can be evaluated only statically through the analysis of the software inner structure, its source code, at the unit level, the technology level and the system level, which is in effect how its architecture adheres to sound principles of software architecture outlined in a paper on the topic by OMG. But some structural qualities, such as usability, can be assessed only dynamically . Other aspects, such as reliability, might involve not only the software but also the underlying hardware, therefore, it can be assessed both statically and dynamically .

Exam Probability: **High**

12. *Answer choices:*

- a. Software assurance
- b. ISO/IEC 9126
- c. Software quality

- d. Software quality assurance

Guidance: level 1

:: Order theory ::

A _____ number is a natural number greater than 1 that cannot be formed by multiplying two smaller natural numbers. A natural number greater than 1 that is not _____ is called a composite number. For example, 5 is _____ because the only ways of writing it as a product, 1×5 or 5×1, involve 5 itself. However, 6 is composite because it is the product of two numbers that are both smaller than 6. _____ s are central in number theory because of the fundamental theorem of arithmetic: every natural number greater than 1 is either a _____ itself or can be factorized as a product of _____ s that is unique up to their order.

Exam Probability: **Low**

13. *Answer choices:*

(see index for correct answer)

- a. Prime
- b. Product order
- c. Bruhat order
- d. Upper set

Guidance: level 1

:: Error detection and correction ::

A _____ is any function that can be used to map data of arbitrary size onto data of a fixed size. The values returned by a _____ are called hash values, hash codes, digests, or simply hashes. _____ s are often used in combination with a hash table, a common data structure used in computer software for rapid data lookup. _____ s accelerate table or database lookup by detecting duplicated records in a large file. One such application is finding similar stretches in DNA sequences. They are also useful in cryptography. A cryptographic _____ allows one to easily verify whether some input data map onto a given hash value, but if the input data is unknown it is deliberately difficult to reconstruct it by knowing the stored hash value. This is used for assuring integrity of transmitted data, and is the building block for HMACs, which provide message authentication.

Exam Probability: **Low**

14. *Answer choices:*

(see index for correct answer)

- a. Chien search
- b. Stop-and-wait ARQ
- c. Locally testable code
- d. Hash function

Guidance: level 1

:: Computer systems ::

In computing, _____ is the sharing of a computing resource among many users by means of multiprogramming and multi-tasking at the same time.

Exam Probability: **Medium**

15. *Answer choices:*

(see index for correct answer)

- a. Computer-aided maintenance
- b. Submarine Command System
- c. Time-sharing
- d. Log analysis

Guidance: level 1

:: Software development philosophies ::

_____ is a software development methodology which is intended to improve software quality and responsiveness to changing customer requirements. As a type of agile software development, it advocates frequent "releases" in short development cycles, which is intended to improve productivity and introduce checkpoints at which new customer requirements can be adopted.

Exam Probability: **Low**

16. *Answer choices:*

(see index for correct answer)

- a. Extreme programming
- b. You aren%27t gonna need it
- c. Comment programming
- d. Cowboy coding

Guidance: level 1

:: Computer graphics ::

In computer science, a _____ is a program that processes its input data to produce output that is used as input to another program. The output is said to be a preprocessed form of the input data, which is often used by some subsequent programs like compilers. The amount and kind of processing done depends on the nature of the _____ ; some _____ s are only capable of performing relatively simple textual substitutions and macro expansions, while others have the power of full-fledged programming languages.

Exam Probability: **High**

17. *Answer choices:*

(see index for correct answer)

- a. Function representation
- b. Preprocessor
- c. Superquadrics
- d. Turtle graphics

:: SPARC microprocessor architecture ::

_____ is a reduced instruction set computing instruction set architecture originally developed by Sun Microsystems. Its design was strongly influenced by the experimental Berkeley RISC system developed in the early 1980s. First released in 1987, _____ was one of the most successful early commercial RISC systems, and its success led to the introduction of similar RISC designs from a number of vendors through the 1980s and 90s.

Exam Probability: **Medium**

18. *Answer choices:*

(see index for correct answer)

- a. Alewife
- b. S1 Core
- c. Visual Instruction Set
- d. LEON

:: Strategy ::

_____ is a high level plan to achieve one or more goals under conditions of uncertainty. In the sense of the "art of the general," which included several subsets of skills including tactics, siegecraft, logistics etc., the term came into use in the 6th century C.E. in East Roman terminology, and was translated into Western vernacular languages only in the 18th century. From then until the 20th century, the word "_____" came to denote "a comprehensive way to try to pursue political ends, including the threat or actual use of force, in a dialectic of wills" in a military conflict, in which both adversaries interact.

Exam Probability: **Low**

19. *Answer choices:*

(see index for correct answer)

- a. Strategic Initiative
- b. Strategy
- c. Institute for the Analysis of Global Security
- d. Divide and rule

Guidance: level 1

:: Distributed computing architecture ::

The _____ is a standard for distributed simulation, used when building a simulation for a larger purpose by combining several simulations. The standard was developed in the 90's under the leadership of the US Department of Defense and was later transitioned to become an open international IEEE standard. It is a recommended standard within NATO through STANAG 4603. Today the HLA is used in a number of domains including defense and security and civilian applications. The architecture specifies the following components.

Exam Probability: **High**

20. *Answer choices:*

(see index for correct answer)

- a. High-level architecture
- b. RM-ODP
- c. Supercomputer architecture
- d. Distributed shared memory

Guidance: level 1

:: Computer security exploits ::

In information security and programming, a _____ , or buffer overrun, is an anomaly where a program, while writing data to a buffer, overruns the buffer's boundary and overwrites adjacent memory locations.

Exam Probability: **Medium**

21. *Answer choices:*

(see index for correct answer)

- a. Reflection attack
- b. Return-oriented programming
- c. Cross-site scripting
- d. Integer overflow

Guidance: level 1

:: Computer programming ::

A _____ is a type of diagram that represents an algorithm, workflow or process. _____ can also be defined as a diagramatic representation of an algorithm .

Exam Probability: **High**

22. *Answer choices:*

(see index for correct answer)

- a. Code Club
- b. OLE DB for OLAP
- c. Perl 6
- d. Software craftsmanship

Guidance: level 1

:: Algorithm description languages ::

_____ is an informal high-level description of the operating principle of a computer program or other algorithm.

Exam Probability: **Low**

23. *Answer choices:*

(see index for correct answer)

- a. PlusCal
- b. Pseudocode
- c. Structured English
- d. Program Design Language

Guidance: level 1

:: Device drivers ::

In computing, a _____ is a computer program that operates or controls a particular type of device that is attached to a computer. A driver provides a software interface to hardware devices, enabling operating systems and other computer programs to access hardware functions without needing to know precise details about the hardware being used.

24. *Answer choices:*

(see index for correct answer)

- a. Broadcast Driver Architecture
- b. Windows User Mode Driver Framework
- c. Airjack
- d. Device driver

Guidance: level 1

:: Graphical user interface elements ::

In computer interface design, a _____ is a graphical control element on which on-screen buttons, icons, menus, or other input or output elements are placed. _____ s are seen in many types of software such as office suites, graphics editors and web browsers. _____ s are usually distinguished from palettes by their integration into the edges of the screen or larger windows, which results in wasted space if too many underpopulated bars are stacked atop each other or interface inefficiency if overloaded bars are placed on small windows.

Exam Probability: **Medium**

25. *Answer choices:*

(see index for correct answer)

- a. Balloon help
- b. Toolbar
- c. Palette window
- d. Window

Guidance: level 1

:: Central processing unit ::

A _____ , also called a central processor or main processor, is the electronic circuitry within a computer that carries out the instructions of a computer program by performing the basic arithmetic, logic, controlling, and input/output operations specified by the instructions. The computer industry has used the term " _____ " at least since the early 1960s. Traditionally, the term "CPU" refers to a processor, more specifically to its processing unit and control unit , distinguishing these core elements of a computer from external components such as main memory and I/O circuitry.

Exam Probability: **High**

26. *Answer choices:*

(see index for correct answer)

- a. Microcontroller
- b. Index register
- c. Microcode
- d. Central processing unit

:: Data structures ::

In computer science, a _____ is a tree data structure in which each node has at most two children, which are referred to as the left child and the right child. A recursive definition using just set theory notions is that a _____ is a tuple , where L and R are _____ s or the empty set and S is a singleton set. Some authors allow the _____ to be the empty set as well.

Exam Probability: **Medium**

27. *Answer choices:*

(see index for correct answer)

- a. Search data structure
- b. data structures
- c. Device tree
- d. Sorted array

:: Computer security exploits ::

_____ is a code injection technique, used to attack data-driven applications, in which malicious SQL statements are inserted into an entry field for execution . _____ must exploit a security vulnerability in an application's software, for example, when user input is either incorrectly filtered for string literal escape characters embedded in SQL statements or user input is not strongly typed and unexpectedly executed. _____ is mostly known as an attack vector for websites but can be used to attack any type of SQL database.

Exam Probability: **Medium**

28. *Answer choices:*

(see index for correct answer)

- a. Frame injection
- b. Login spoofing
- c. SQL injection
- d. Pre-play attack

Guidance: level 1

:: Data structures ::

In computer science, _____ means that a group of elements is accessed in a predetermined, ordered sequence. _____ is sometimes the only way of accessing the data, for example if it is on a tape. It may also be the access method of choice, for example if all that is wanted is to process a sequence of data elements in order.

29. *Answer choices:*

(see index for correct answer)

- a. Sequential access
- b. Order-maintenance problem
- c. Serialization
- d. Anatree

Guidance: level 1

:: Formal methods ::

_____ is the linguistic and philosophical study of meaning, in language, programming languages, formal logics, and semiotics. It is concerned with the relationship between signifiers—like words, phrases, signs, and symbols—and what they stand for in reality, their denotation.

30. *Answer choices:*

(see index for correct answer)

- a. Mondex
- b. Statistical static timing analysis
- c. Assertion

- d. Semantics

Guidance: level 1

:: Character encoding ::

_____ is a computing industry standard for the consistent encoding, representation, and handling of text expressed in most of the world's writing systems. The standard is maintained by the _____ Consortium, and as of May 2019 the most recent version, _____ 12.1, contains a repertoire of 137,994 characters covering 150 modern and historic scripts, as well as multiple symbol sets and emoji. The character repertoire of the _____ Standard is synchronized with ISO/IEC 10646, and both are code-for-code identical.

Exam Probability: **Low**

31. *Answer choices:*

(see index for correct answer)

- a. Unicode
- b. Baudot code
- c. Vietnamese Quoted-Readable
- d. CCSID

Guidance: level 1

:: Metadata ::

An _____ is a name that identifies either a unique object or a unique class of objects, where the "object" or class may be an idea, physical [countable] object , or physical [noncountable] substance . The abbreviation ID often refers to identity, identification , or an _____ . An _____ may be a word, number, letter, symbol, or any combination of those.

Exam Probability: **High**

32. *Answer choices:*

(see index for correct answer)

- a. File association
- b. Tag
- c. Metadata discovery
- d. Identifier

Guidance: level 1

:: Abstraction ::

_____ is the state or quality of being simple. Something easy to understand or explain seems simple, in contrast to something complicated. Alternatively, as Herbert A. Simon suggests, something is simple or complex depending on the way we choose to describe it. In some uses, the label "_____ " can imply beauty, purity, or clarity. In other cases, the term may occur with negative connotations to suggest, a deficit or insufficiency of nuance or of complexity of a thing, relative to what one supposes as required.

Exam Probability: **High**

33. *Answer choices:*

(see index for correct answer)

- a. Entitativity
- b. Abstract and concrete
- c. Logical form
- d. Simplicity

Guidance: level 1

:: World Wide Web Consortium standards ::

Hypertext Markup Language is the standard markup language for creating web pages and web applications. With Cascading Style Sheets and JavaScript, it forms a triad of cornerstone technologies for the World Wide Web.

Exam Probability: **High**

34. *Answer choices:*

- a. XQuery Update Facility
- b. Message Transmission Optimization Mechanism
- c. Natural Language Semantics Markup Language
- d. Device Description Repository

Guidance: level 1

:: Data security ::

In computer science, _____ is the process of ensuring data have undergone data cleansing to ensure they have data quality, that is, that they are both correct and useful. It uses routines, often called "validation rules" "validation constraints" or "check routines", that check for correctness, meaningfulness, and security of data that are input to the system. The rules may be implemented through the automated facilities of a data dictionary, or by the inclusion of explicit application program validation logic.

Exam Probability: **Low**

35. *Answer choices:*

- a. Secure Network
- b. Relocatable user backup
- c. Data validation

- d. Actiance

Guidance: level 1

:: Software engineering ::

A _____ is a system on intercommunicating components based on software forming part of a computer system . It "consists of a number of separate programs, configuration files, which are used to set up these programs, system documentation, which describes the structure of the system, and user documentation, which explains how to use the system".

Exam Probability: **Low**

36. *Answer choices:*

(see index for correct answer)

- a. Software system
- b. Experimental software engineering
- c. System requirements specification
- d. Frame technology

Guidance: level 1

:: Programming paradigms ::

_____ is a programming paradigm based on the concept of "objects", which can contain data, in the form of fields , and code, in the form of procedures . A feature of objects is an object's procedures that can access and often modify the data fields of the object with which they are associated . In OOP, computer programs are designed by making them out of objects that interact with one another. OOP languages are diverse, but the most popular ones are class-based, meaning that objects are instances of classes, which also determine their types.

Exam Probability: **Low**

37. *Answer choices:*

(see index for correct answer)

- a. procedural programming
- b. Object-oriented programming

Guidance: level 1

:: Client-server database management systems ::

_____ is an open-source relational database management system . Its name is a combination of "My", the name of co-founder Michael Widenius's daughter, and "SQL", the abbreviation for Structured Query Language.

Exam Probability: **High**

38. *Answer choices:*

(see index for correct answer)

- a. MariaDB
- b. MySQL
- c. Transbase

Guidance: level 1

:: Usability ::

_____ is the ease of use and learnability of a human-made object such as a tool or device. In software engineering, _____ is the degree to which a software can be used by specified consumers to achieve quantified objectives with effectiveness, efficiency, and satisfaction in a quantified context of use.

Exam Probability: **Low**

39. *Answer choices:*

(see index for correct answer)

- a. Attitudinal analytics
- b. User journey
- c. Component-based usability testing
- d. Jaime Levy

Guidance: level 1

:: Philosophical logic ::

_____ is the pattern of narrative development that aims to make vivid a place, object, character, or group. _____ is one of four rhetorical modes , along with exposition, argumentation, and narration. In practice it would be difficult to write literature that drew on just one of the four basic modes.

Exam Probability: **High**

40. *Answer choices:*

(see index for correct answer)

- a. Rigour
- b. Fitch-style calculus
- c. Philosophical logic
- d. Description

Guidance: level 1

:: Bit data structures ::

In computing, a _____ is a mapping from some domain to bits. It is also called a bit array or _____ index.

Exam Probability: **High**

41. *Answer choices:*

(see index for correct answer)

- a. Bit plane
- b. Bit field
- c. Bitmap

Guidance: level 1

:: Machine code ::

In computing, _____ or object module is the product of a compiler. In a general sense _____ is a sequence of statements or instructions in a computer language, usually a machine code language or an intermediate language such as register transfer language . The term indicates that the code is the goal or result of the compiling process, with some early sources referring to source code as a "subject program."

Exam Probability: **Low**

42. *Answer choices:*

(see index for correct answer)

- a. Object code
- b. Code generation
- c. Code injection
- d. Operand

:: Software engineering ::

_____ is the application of engineering to the development of software in a systematic method.

Exam Probability: **Low**

43. *Answer choices:*

(see index for correct answer)

- a. System appreciation
- b. ISO/IEC JTC 1/SC 7
- c. Software construction
- d. Software visualization

Guidance: level 1

:: Educational programming languages ::

A _____ is a physiological capacity of organisms that provides data for perception. The _____ s and their operation, classification, and theory are overlapping topics studied by a variety of fields, most notably neuroscience, cognitive psychology , and philosophy of perception. The nervous system has a specific sensory nervous system, and a _____ organ, or sensor, dedicated to each _____ .

Exam Probability: **High**

44. *Answer choices:*

(see index for correct answer)

- a. Sense
- b. TouchDevelop
- c. Object-Oriented Turing
- d. Phrogram

Guidance: level 1

:: Software testing ::

A _____ is a specification of the inputs, execution conditions, testing procedure, and expected results that define a single test to be executed to achieve a particular software testing objective, such as to exercise a particular program path or to verify compliance with a specific requirement. _____ s underlie testing that is methodical rather than haphazard. A battery of _____ s can be built to produce the desired coverage of the software being tested. Formally defined _____ s allow the same tests to be run repeatedly against successive versions of the software, allowing for effective and consistent regression testing.

Exam Probability: **Medium**

45. *Answer choices:*

(see index for correct answer)

- a. Bebugging
- b. A/B testing
- c. Test case
- d. Model-based testing

Guidance: level 1

:: Usability ::

In the performing arts, a _____ is a synoptical collage of an event or series of actions and events. In the commedia dell`arte it was an outline of entrances, exits, and action describing the plot of a play, and was literally pinned to the back of the scenery. It is also known as canovaccio or "that which is pinned to the canvas" of which the scenery was constructed.

46. *Answer choices:*

(see index for correct answer)

- a. Scenario
- b. User analysis
- c. Flexibility-usability tradeoff
- d. Jaime Levy

Guidance: level 1

:: Software testing ::

_____ is testing conducted on a complete integrated system to evaluate the system's compliance with its specified requirements.

Exam Probability: **High**

47. *Answer choices:*

(see index for correct answer)

- a. Load testing
- b. Test management
- c. Black-box testing
- d. Pychecker

:: Data management ::

A _____ , or metadata repository, as defined in the IBM Dictionary of Computing, is a "centralized repository of information about data such as meaning, relationships to other data, origin, usage, and format". Oracle defines it as a collection of tables with metadata. The term can have one of several closely related meanings pertaining to databases and database management systems .

Exam Probability: **High**

48. *Answer choices:*

(see index for correct answer)

- a. Data monetization
- b. Data architecture
- c. Data dictionary
- d. Data conditioning

:: Programming libraries ::

A _____ in computer programming is the library made available across implementations of a programming language. These libraries are conventionally described in programming language specifications; however, contents of a language's associated library may also be determined by more informal practices of a language's community.

Exam Probability: **High**

49. *Answer choices:*

(see index for correct answer)

- a. OpenSC
- b. Standard library

Guidance: level 1

:: Computer graphics ::

An _____ is an artifact that depicts visual perception, such as a photograph or other two-dimensional picture, that resembles a subject—usually a physical object—and thus provides a depiction of it. In the context of signal processing, an _____ is a distributed amplitude of color.

Exam Probability: **Low**

50. *Answer choices:*

(see index for correct answer)

- a. Portal rendering
- b. Image
- c. Retained mode
- d. CityEngine

Guidance: level 1

:: Systems analysis ::

A _____ in software engineering and organizational theory is a chart which shows the breakdown of a system to its lowest manageable levels. They are used in structured programming to arrange program modules into a tree. Each module is represented by a box, which contains the module's name. The tree structure visualizes the relationships between modules.

Exam Probability: **Medium**

51. *Answer choices:*

(see index for correct answer)

- a. Structure chart
- b. Failure mode and effects analysis
- c. Functional flow block diagram
- d. Diakoptics

Guidance: level 1

:: Naming conventions ::

_____ is an identifier naming convention in computer programming, in which the name of a variable or function indicates its intention or kind, and in some dialects its type. The original _____ uses intention or kind in its naming convention and is sometimes called Apps Hungarian as it became popular in the Microsoft Apps division in the development of Word, Excel and other apps. As the Microsoft Windows division adopted the naming convention, they used the actual data type for naming, and this convention became widely spread through the Windows API; this is sometimes called Systems _____ .

Exam Probability: **Low**

52. *Answer choices:*

(see index for correct answer)

- a. namespace
- b. Leszynski naming convention

Guidance: level 1

:: Instruction set architectures ::

_____ is a reduced instruction set computing instruction set architecture created by the 1991 Apple–IBM–Motorola alliance, known as AIM. _____ , as an evolving instruction set, has since 2006 been named Power ISA, while the old name lives on as a trademark for some implementations of Power Architecture-based processors.

53. *Answer choices:*

(see index for correct answer)

- a. PowerPC
- b. Itanium

Guidance: level 1

:: Digital typography ::

_____ is a page description language in the electronic publishing and desktop publishing business. It is a dynamically typed, concatenative programming language and was created at Adobe Systems by John Warnock, Charles Geschke, Doug Brotz, Ed Taft and Bill Paxton from 1982 to 1984.

Exam Probability: **High**

54. *Answer choices:*

(see index for correct answer)

- a. Computer font
- b. Postscript
- c. Font management software
- d. Interpress

:: Trees (data structures) ::

In computer science, _____ is a form of graph traversal and refers to the process of visiting each node in a tree data structure, exactly once. Such traversals are classified by the order in which the nodes are visited. The following algorithms are described for a binary tree, but they may be generalized to other trees as well.

Exam Probability: **Low**

55. *Answer choices:*

(see index for correct answer)

- a. Doubly chained tree
- b. Trace tree
- c. Radix tree
- d. Node

:: Computing input devices ::

In computing, an _____ is a piece of computer hardware equipment used to provide data and control signals to an information processing system such as a computer or information appliance. Examples of _____ s include keyboards, mouse, scanners, digital cameras and joysticks. Audio _____ s may be used for purposes including speech recognition. Many companies are utilizing speech recognition to help assist users to use their device.

Exam Probability: **High**

56. *Answer choices:*

(see index for correct answer)

- a. Griffin PowerMate
- b. Input device
- c. Microphone
- d. 3D scanner

Guidance: level 1

:: Software development ::

_____ is the process of conceiving, specifying, designing, programming, documenting, testing, and bug fixing involved in creating and maintaining applications, frameworks, or other software components. _____ is a process of writing and maintaining the source code, but in a broader sense, it includes all that is involved between the conception of the desired software through to the final manifestation of the software, sometimes in a planned and structured process. Therefore, _____ may include research, new development, prototyping, modification, reuse, re-engineering, maintenance, or any other activities that result in software products.

Exam Probability: **Medium**

57. *Answer choices:*

(see index for correct answer)

- a. Mendix
- b. VersaPay
- c. Custom software developer
- d. Software development

Guidance: level 1

:: Data management ::

_____ is "data [information] that provides information about other data". Many distinct types of _____ exist, among these descriptive _____, structural _____, administrative _____, reference _____ and statistical _____.

58. *Answer choices:*

(see index for correct answer)

- a. White pages schema
- b. Metadata
- c. Automatic data processing equipment
- d. Match report

Guidance: level 1

:: Virtual reality ::

Open Graphics Library is a cross-language, cross-platform application programming interface for rendering 2D and 3D vector graphics. The API is typically used to interact with a graphics processing unit , to achieve hardware-accelerated rendering.

Exam Probability: **High**

59. *Answer choices:*

(see index for correct answer)

- a. Lifelike experience
- b. Oculus Rift
- c. XVRML

- d. OpenGL

Guidance: level 1

Computer security

Computer security, cybersecurity or information technology security (IT security) is the protection of computer systems from theft or damage to their hardware, software or electronic data, as well as from disruption or misdirection of the services they provide.

:: Malware ::

In distributed computing, code mobility is the ability for running programs, code or objects to be migrated from one machine or application to another. This is the process of moving _____ across the nodes of a network as opposed to distributed computation where the data is moved.

1. *Answer choices:*

(see index for correct answer)

- a. Your PC Protector
- b. Warhol worm
- c. Logic bomb
- d. Typhoid adware

Guidance: level 1

:: Application layer protocols ::

The _____ is a communication protocol for electronic mail transmission. As an Internet standard, SMTP was first defined in 1982 by RFC 821, and updated in 2008 by RFC 5321 to Extended SMTP additions, which is the protocol variety in widespread use today. Mail servers and other message transfer agents use SMTP to send and receive mail messages. Proprietary systems such as Microsoft Exchange and IBM Notes and webmail systems such as Outlook.com, Gmail and Yahoo! Mail may use non-standard protocols internally, but all use SMTP when sending to or receiving email from outside their own systems. SMTP servers commonly use the Transmission Control Protocol on port number 25.

Exam Probability: **High**

2. *Answer choices:*

(see index for correct answer)

- a. File Access Listener
- b. Application layer
- c. Simple Mail Transfer Protocol
- d. Discard Protocol

Guidance: level 1

:: Computer network security ::

_____ is a security algorithm for IEEE 802.11 wireless networks. Introduced as part of the original 802.11 standard ratified in 1997, its intention was to provide data confidentiality comparable to that of a traditional wired network. WEP, recognizable by its key of 10 or 26 hexadecimal digits , was at one time widely in use and was often the first security choice presented to users by router configuration tools.

Exam Probability: **Low**

3. *Answer choices:*

(see index for correct answer)

- a. Credant Technologies
- b. Knowledge-based authentication
- c. Cisco PIX
- d. Virtual private server

Guidance: level 1

:: Transmission Control Protocol ::

The _____ is one of the main protocols of the Internet protocol suite. It originated in the initial network implementation in which it complemented the Internet Protocol . Therefore, the entire suite is commonly referred to as TCP/IP. TCP provides reliable, ordered, and error-checked delivery of a stream of octets between applications running on hosts communicating via an IP network. Major internet applications such as the World Wide Web, email, remote administration, and file transfer rely on TCP. Applications that do not require reliable data stream service may use the User Datagram Protocol , which provides a connectionless datagram service that emphasizes reduced latency over reliability.

Exam Probability: **Medium**

4. *Answer choices:*

(see index for correct answer)

- a. T/TCP
- b. Compound TCP
- c. Congestion window
- d. Obfuscated TCP

Guidance: level 1

:: Virtual reality ::

The _____ is the global system of interconnected computer networks that use the _____ protocol suite to link devices worldwide. It is a network of networks that consists of private, public, academic, business, and government networks of local to global scope, linked by a broad array of electronic, wireless, and optical networking technologies. The _____ carries a vast range of information resources and services, such as the inter-linked hypertext documents and applications of the World Wide Web, electronic mail, telephony, and file sharing.

Exam Probability: **Low**

5. *Answer choices:*

(see index for correct answer)

- a. V-business
- b. Internet
- c. TreadPort Active Wind Tunnel
- d. Visroom

Guidance: level 1

:: Computer security procedures ::

_____ is the identification of an organization's assets, followed by the development, documentation, and implementation of policies and procedures for protecting these assets.

Exam Probability: **Medium**

6. *Answer choices:*

(see index for correct answer)

- a. Security management
- b. National Information Assurance Certification and Accreditation Process
- c. DShield
- d. Mobile device forensics

Guidance: level 1

:: Computer systems ::

A _____ , or sysadmin, is a person who is responsible for the upkeep, configuration, and reliable operation of computer systems; especially multi-user computers, such as servers. The _____ seeks to ensure that the uptime, performance, resources, and security of the computers they manage meet the needs of the users, without exceeding a set budget when doing so.

Exam Probability: **Low**

7. *Answer choices:*

(see index for correct answer)

- a. Problem solving environment
- b. Operability
- c. Computer-aided maintenance

- d. System administrator

Guidance: level 1

:: Computer security models ::

In computer security, _____ is a complex access control model based on the interaction between any combination of objects and subjects .

Exam Probability: **Medium**

8. *Answer choices:*

(see index for correct answer)

- a. Type enforcement
- b. Brewer and Nash model
- c. Lattice-based access control
- d. Role-based access control

Guidance: level 1

:: Cryptography ::

_____ or cryptology is the practice and study of techniques for secure communication in the presence of third parties called adversaries. More generally, _____ is about constructing and analyzing protocols that prevent third parties or the public from reading private messages; various aspects in information security such as data confidentiality, data integrity, authentication, and non-repudiation are central to modern _____ . Modern _____ exists at the intersection of the disciplines of mathematics, computer science, electrical engineering, communication science, and physics. Applications of _____ include electronic commerce, chip-based payment cards, digital currencies, computer passwords, and military communications.

Exam Probability: **Low**

9. *Answer choices:*

(see index for correct answer)

- a. Cryptography
- b. Cryptographic Module Testing Laboratory
- c. End-to-end encryption
- d. Blacker

Guidance: level 1

:: Data recovery ::

_____ is a data recovery software developed by Runtime Software. It can be used to recover data from external and internal hard disks, in the FAT and the NTFS file systems, although different variants of the program are needed for each file system. Registration of the software is required in order to recover data with the software.

Exam Probability: **High**

10. *Answer choices:*

(see index for correct answer)

- a. WinHex
- b. Disk Drill Basic
- c. SystemRescueCD
- d. DataNumen Word Repair

Guidance: level 1

:: Cryptographic protocols ::

The _____ is an Internet protocol used for obtaining the revocation status of an X.509 digital certificate. It is described in RFC 6960 and is on the Internet standards track. It was created as an alternative to certificate revocation lists , specifically addressing certain problems associated with using CRLs in a public key infrastructure . Messages communicated via OCSP are encoded in ASN.1 and are usually communicated over HTTP. The "request/response" nature of these messages leads to OCSP servers being termed OCSP responders.

11. *Answer choices:*

(see index for correct answer)

- a. Private information retrieval
- b. SPNEGO
- c. Online Certificate Status Protocol
- d. Key exchange

Guidance: level 1

:: Data security ::

> Single-loss expectancy is the monetary value expected from the occurrence of a risk on an asset. It is related to risk management and risk assessment.

Exam Probability: **High**

12. *Answer choices:*

(see index for correct answer)

- a. Relocatable user backup
- b. Administrative share
- c. Sheep dip
- d. Computer recycling

:: Data security ::

ISACA is an international professional association focused on IT governance. On its IRS filings, it is known as the Information Systems Audit and Control Association, although ISACA now goes by its acronym only.

Exam Probability: **Medium**

13. *Answer choices:*

(see index for correct answer)

- a. Certified Information Systems Auditor
- b. Budapest Declaration on Machine Readable Travel Documents
- c. Asset
- d. Password fatigue

:: Internet fraud ::

_____ is the act of using a computer to take or alter electronic data, or to gain unlawful use of a computer or system. In the United States, _____ is specifically proscribed by the _____ and Abuse Act, which criminalizes computer-related acts under federal jurisdiction. Types of _____ include.

Exam Probability: **Medium**

14. *Answer choices:*

(see index for correct answer)

- a. Russian Business Network
- b. Adversarial information retrieval
- c. Computer fraud
- d. Artists Against 419

Guidance: level 1

:: Computer security procedures ::

_____ and setgid are Unix access rights flags that allow users to run an executable with the permissions of the executable's owner or group respectively and to change behaviour in directories. They are often used to allow users on a computer system to run programs with temporarily elevated privileges in order to perform a specific task. While the assumed user id or group id privileges provided are not always elevated, at a minimum they are specific.

15. *Answer choices:*

(see index for correct answer)

- a. Intruder detection
- b. Protection Profile
- c. Not Just Another Bogus List
- d. Privilege revocation

Guidance: level 1

:: Application layer protocols ::

_____ is an Internet Standard protocol for collecting and organizing information about managed devices on IP networks and for modifying that information to change device behavior. Devices that typically support SNMP include cable modems, routers, switches, servers, workstations, printers, and more.

Exam Probability: **Medium**

16. *Answer choices:*

(see index for correct answer)

- a. Service discovery
- b. Simple Mail Transfer Protocol

- c. Tabular Data Stream
- d. Simple Network Management Protocol

Guidance: level 1

:: Software add-ons ::

_____ is a software framework created by Microsoft that adapts its earlier Component Object Model and Object Linking and Embedding technologies for content downloaded from a network, particularly from the World Wide Web. Microsoft introduced _____ in 1996. In principle, _____ is not dependent on Microsoft Windows operating systems, but in practice, most _____ controls only run on Windows. Most also require the client to be running on an x86-based computer because _____ controls contain compiled code.

Exam Probability: **Low**

17. *Answer choices:*

(see index for correct answer)

- a. Adlesse
- b. Google Chrome Extensions
- c. MediaWiki extension
- d. ActiveX

Guidance: level 1

:: Network analyzers ::

_____ is a computer networking utility for reading from and writing to network connections using TCP or UDP. The command is designed to be a dependable back-end that can be used directly or easily driven by other programs and scripts. At the same time, it is a feature-rich network debugging and investigation tool, since it can produce almost any kind of connection its user could need and has a number of built-in capabilities.

Exam Probability: **Low**

18. *Answer choices:*

(see index for correct answer)

- a. SNMPTT
- b. Netcat
- c. Network weathermap
- d. Pcap

Guidance: level 1

:: Computer network security ::

Terminal Access Controller Access-Control System refers to a family of related protocols handling remote authentication and related services for networked access control through a centralized server. The original _____ protocol, which dates back to 1984, was used for communicating with an authentication server, common in older UNIX networks; it spawned related protocols.

Exam Probability: **High**

19. *Answer choices:*

(see index for correct answer)

- a. Ticket
- b. TeamF1
- c. TACACS
- d. Cisco Systems VPN Client

Guidance: level 1

:: Computer security exploits ::

A _____ is a form of network attack in which a valid data transmission is maliciously or fraudulently repeated or delayed. This is carried out either by the originator or by an adversary who intercepts the data and re-transmits it, possibly as part of a masquerade attack by IP packet substitution. This is one of the lower tier versions of a "Man-in-the-middle attack".

Exam Probability: **High**

(see index for correct answer)

20. *Answer choices:*

- a. Frame injection
- b. Pass the hash
- c. Replay attack
- d. Heap spraying

Guidance: level 1

:: Cryptography ::

A _____ is a special class of hash function that has certain properties which make it suitable for use in cryptography. It is a mathematical algorithm that maps data of arbitrary size to a bit string of a fixed size and is designed to be a one-way function, that is, a function which is infeasible to invert. The only way to recreate the input data from an ideal _____`s output is to attempt a brute-force search of possible inputs to see if they produce a match, or use a rainbow table of matched hashes. Bruce Schneier has called one-way hash functions "the workhorses of modern cryptography".The input data is often called the message, and the output is often called the message digest or simply the digest.

Exam Probability: **Low**

21. *Answer choices:*

(see index for correct answer)

- a. Knapsack problem

- b. Cryptographic hash function
- c. Export of cryptography in the United States
- d. Frederick Edward Hulme

Guidance: level 1

:: Computer systems ::

In computer log management and intelligence, _____ is an art and science seeking to make sense out of computer-generated records . The process of creating such records is called data logging.

Exam Probability: **Low**

22. *Answer choices:*

(see index for correct answer)

- a. Electronic logbook
- b. Log analysis
- c. Software metering
- d. Operability

Guidance: level 1

:: Computer security exploits ::

_____ is a code injection technique, used to attack data-driven applications, in which malicious SQL statements are inserted into an entry field for execution . _____ must exploit a security vulnerability in an application's software, for example, when user input is either incorrectly filtered for string literal escape characters embedded in SQL statements or user input is not strongly typed and unexpectedly executed. _____ is mostly known as an attack vector for websites but can be used to attack any type of SQL database.

Exam Probability: **High**

23. *Answer choices:*

(see index for correct answer)

- a. FTP bounce attack
- b. Cross-application scripting
- c. Laptop theft
- d. SQL injection

Guidance: level 1

:: Portable software ::

_____ is a free and open-source password manager program for use with Microsoft Windows.

Exam Probability: **Low**

24. *Answer choices:*

(see index for correct answer)

- a. Psi
- b. Frets on Fire
- c. Freeseer
- d. Windows Post-Install Wizard

Guidance: level 1

:: Unix programming tools ::

_____ is a family of two high-level, general-purpose, interpreted, dynamic programming languages. " _____ " usually refers to _____ 5, but it may also refer to its redesigned "sister language", _____ 6.

Exam Probability: **Low**

25. *Answer choices:*

(see index for correct answer)

- a. Size
- b. Lipog
- c. Genius
- d. Sweble

Guidance: level 1

:: Semantic Web ::

In cryptography, a _____ is a concept used in PGP, GnuPG, and other OpenPGP-compatible systems to establish the authenticity of the binding between a public key and its owner. Its decentralized trust model is an alternative to the centralized trust model of a public key infrastructure , which relies exclusively on a certificate authority . As with computer networks, there are many independent webs of trust, and any user can be a part of, and a link between, multiple webs.

Exam Probability: **Medium**

26. *Answer choices:*

(see index for correct answer)

- a. Web of trust
- b. Controlled vocabulary
- c. PROTON
- d. Eureqa

Guidance: level 1

:: Computer network security ::

In cryptography, a _____ is part of a cryptosystem intended to reduce the risks inherent in exchanging keys. KDCs often operate in systems within which some users may have permission to use certain services at some times and not at others.

27. *Answer choices:*

(see index for correct answer)

- a. SonicWall
- b. BNC
- c. Stateful firewall
- d. Key distribution center

Guidance: level 1

:: Side channel attacks ::

In cryptography, a _____ is a side channel attack in which the attacker attempts to compromise a cryptosystem by analyzing the time taken to execute cryptographic algorithms. Every logical operation in a computer takes time to execute, and the time can differ based on the input; with precise measurements of the time for each operation, an attacker can work backwards to the input.

28. *Answer choices:*

(see index for correct answer)

- a. Acoustic cryptanalysis
- b. Timing attack
- c. DMA attack
- d. Differential fault analysis

Guidance: level 1

:: Computer access control protocols ::

The _____ , also known as Protected EAP or simply PEAP, is a protocol that encapsulates the Extensible Authentication Protocol within an encrypted and authenticated Transport Layer Security tunnel. The purpose was to correct deficiencies in EAP; EAP assumed a protected communication channel, such as that provided by physical security, so facilities for protection of the EAP conversation were not provided.

Exam Probability: **Low**

29. *Answer choices:*

(see index for correct answer)

- a. Remote Authentication Dial In User Service
- b. LAN Manager
- c. ID-MM7
- d. Protected Extensible Authentication Protocol

:: Computer security models ::

_____ or multiple levels of security is the application of a computer system to process information with incompatible classifications , permit access by users with different security clearances and needs-to-know, and prevent users from obtaining access to information for which they lack authorization. There are two contexts for the use of _____ . One is to refer to a system that is adequate to protect itself from subversion and has robust mechanisms to separate information domains, that is, trustworthy. Another context is to refer to an application of a computer that will require the computer to be strong enough to protect itself from subversion and possess adequate mechanisms to separate information domains, that is, a system we must trust. This distinction is important because systems that need to be trusted are not necessarily trustworthy.

Exam Probability: **Low**

30. *Answer choices:*

(see index for correct answer)

- a. Graham-Denning model
- b. Multilevel security
- c. Lattice-based access control
- d. HRU

:: Programming language implementation ::

In computing, a _____ is an emulation of a computer system. _____ s are based on computer architectures and provide functionality of a physical computer. Their implementations may involve specialized hardware, software, or a combination.

Exam Probability: **High**

31. *Answer choices:*

(see index for correct answer)

- a. General-purpose macro processor
- b. Translator
- c. Virtual machine
- d. Undefined behavior

Guidance: level 1

:: Computer network security ::

A _____ is an application which controls network traffic to and from a computer, permitting or denying communications based on a security policy. Typically it works as an application layer firewall.

Exam Probability: **Medium**

32. *Answer choices:*

(see index for correct answer)

- a. Web application security scanner
- b. NetScreen Technologies
- c. Personal firewall
- d. Cloudvpn

Guidance: level 1

:: Computer security ::

In the fields of physical security and information security, _____ is the selective restriction of access to a place or other resource. The act of accessing may mean consuming, entering, or using. Permission to access a resource is called authorization.

Exam Probability: **Low**

33. *Answer choices:*

(see index for correct answer)

- a. Cracking of wireless networks
- b. Access control
- c. Committee on National Security Systems
- d. Principal

:: Computer security ::

An intrusion detection system is a device or software application that monitors a network or systems for malicious activity or policy violations. Any malicious activity or violation is typically reported either to an administrator or collected centrally using a security information and event management system. A SIEM system combines outputs from multiple sources, and uses alarm filtering techniques to distinguish malicious activity from false alarms.

Exam Probability: **Low**

34. *Answer choices:*

(see index for correct answer)

- a. Sherwood Applied Business Security Architecture
- b. Host Based Security System
- c. Cyber Intelligence Sharing and Protection Act
- d. Intrusion prevention system

:: Cryptographic protocols ::

In computing, Internet Protocol Security is a secure network protocol suite that authenticates and encrypts the packets of data sent over an Internet Protocol network. It is used in virtual private networks .

Exam Probability: **Medium**

35. *Answer choices:*

(see index for correct answer)

- a. IPsec
- b. Datagram Transport Layer Security
- c. Secure Real-time Transport Protocol
- d. Microsoft Point-to-Point Encryption

Guidance: level 1

:: Computer security exploits ::

In cryptanalysis and computer security, _____ is the process of recovering passwords from data that have been stored in or transmitted by a computer system. A common approach is to try guesses repeatedly for the password and check them against an available cryptographic hash of the password.

Exam Probability: **Low**

36. *Answer choices:*

(see index for correct answer)

- a. Password cracking
- b. Buffer overflow
- c. Cross-site scripting
- d. JIT spraying

Guidance: level 1

:: Computer network security ::

_____ is an approach to computer security that attempts to unify endpoint security technology , user or system authentication and network security enforcement.

Exam Probability: **Low**

37. *Answer choices:*

(see index for correct answer)

- a. Sality
- b. Verisys
- c. RedSeal Networks
- d. Network Access Control

Guidance: level 1

:: Computer access control ::

_____ , also known as content protection, copy prevention and copy restriction, is any effort designed to prevent the reproduction of software, films, music, and other media, usually for copyright reasons. Various methods have been devised to prevent reproduction so that companies will gain benefit from each person who obtains an authorized copy of their product. Unauthorized copying and distribution accounted for $2.4 billion in lost revenue in the United States alone in the 1990s, and is assumed to be causing impact on revenues in the music and the game industry, leading to proposal of stricter copyright laws such as PIPA. Some methods of _____ have also led to criticisms because it caused inconvenience for honest consumers, or it secretly installed additional or unwanted software to detect copying activities on the consumer's computer. Making _____ effective while protecting consumer rights is still an ongoing problem with media publication.

Exam Probability: **High**

38. *Answer choices:*

(see index for correct answer)

- a. Mobilegov
- b. Salute picture
- c. Initiative For Open Authentication
- d. Copy protection

Guidance: level 1

:: Cryptography ::

In cryptography, _____ or cyphertext is the result of encryption performed on plaintext using an algorithm, called a cipher. _____ is also known as encrypted or encoded information because it contains a form of the original plaintext that is unreadable by a human or computer without the proper cipher to decrypt it. Decryption, the inverse of encryption, is the process of turning _____ into readable plaintext. _____ is not to be confused with codetext because the latter is a result of a code, not a cipher.

Exam Probability: **Low**

39. *Answer choices:*

(see index for correct answer)

- a. NIPRNet
- b. Communications security
- c. Ciphertext
- d. Cryptocurrency

Guidance: level 1

:: Computer forensics ::

The _____ credential demonstrates competency in computer forensics. The CCE is offered by the International Society for Computer Examiners , an organization that hopes to create and maintain high standards for computer examiners worldwide.

Exam Probability: **Medium**

40. *Answer choices:*

(see index for correct answer)

- a. Certified Computer Examiner
- b. Device configuration overlay
- c. Selective file dumper
- d. Anti-computer forensics

Guidance: level 1

:: Cryptography ::

In the mathematics of the real numbers, the logarithm logb a is a number x such that bx = a, for given numbers a and b. Analogously, in any group G, powers bk can be defined for all integers k, and the _____ logb a is an integer k such that bk = a. In number theory, the more commonly used term is index: we can write x = indr a for rx = a if r is a primitive root of m and gcd = 1.

Exam Probability: **High**

41. *Answer choices:*

(see index for correct answer)

- a. Password psychology
- b. Discrete logarithm
- c. Multiple encryption
- d. Zerocoin

:: Malware ::

_____ is any software intentionally designed to cause damage to a computer, server, client, or computer network. _____ does the damage after it is implanted or introduced in some way into a target's computer and can take the form of executable code, scripts, active content, and other software. The code is described as computer viruses, worms, Trojan horses, ransomware, spyware, adware, and scareware, among other terms. _____ has a malicious intent, acting against the interest of the computer user—and so does not include software that causes unintentional harm due to some deficiency, which is typically described as a software bug.

Exam Probability: **Medium**

42. *Answer choices:*

(see index for correct answer)

- a. Malware
- b. Cyberweapon
- c. Dialer
- d. Spy-phishing

:: Computer network security ::

In computer networking, _____ is a technique used to ensure that incoming packets are actually from the networks from which they claim to originate. This can be used as a countermeasure against various spoofing attacks where the attacker's packets contain fake IP addresses to make it difficult to find the source of the attack. This technique is often used in the denial-of-service attack, and this is a primary target of _____ .

Exam Probability: **High**

43. *Answer choices:*

- a. Captive portal
- b. Port forwarding
- c. Open proxy
- d. Verisys

Guidance: level 1

:: Software testing ::

A 1964 paper entitled Program Management in Design and Development used the term _____ s and defined it as "a team of undomesticated and uninhibited technical specialists, selected for their experience, energy, and imagination, and assigned to track down relentlessly every possible source of failure in a spacecraft subsystem". The paper consists of anecdotes and answers to questions from a panel on improving issues in program management concerning testing and quality assurance in aerospace vehicle development and production. One of the authors was Walter C. Williams, an engineer at the Manned Spacecraft Center and part of the Edwards Air Force Base National Advisory Committee for Aeronautics. Williams suggests that _____ s are an effective and useful method for advancing the reliability of systems and subsystems in the context of actual flight environments.

Exam Probability: **Low**

44. *Answer choices:*

(see index for correct answer)

- a. Tiger team
- b. Stream X-Machine
- c. Functionality assurance
- d. Month of bugs

Guidance: level 1

:: Risk analysis ::

_____ is the identification, evaluation, and prioritization of risks followed by coordinated and economical application of resources to minimize, monitor, and control the probability or impact of unfortunate events or to maximize the realization of opportunities.

Exam Probability: **Medium**

45. *Answer choices:*

(see index for correct answer)

- a. Accident
- b. Core damage frequency
- c. Litigation risk analysis
- d. Factor analysis of information risk

Guidance: level 1

:: Computer security ::

_____ , also called back engineering, is the process by which a man-made object is deconstructed to reveal its designs, architecture, or to extract knowledge from the object; similar to scientific research, the only difference being that scientific research is about a natural phenomenon.

Exam Probability: **Low**

46. *Answer choices:*

(see index for correct answer)

- a. Physical access
- b. Parkerian Hexad
- c. Privileged Identity Management
- d. Reverse engineering

Guidance: level 1

:: Computer security models ::

In computer systems security, _____ or role-based security is an approach to restricting system access to unauthorized users. It is used by the majority of enterprises with more than 500 employees, and can implement mandatory access control or discretionary access control .

Exam Probability: **High**

47. *Answer choices:*

(see index for correct answer)

- a. Capability-based security
- b. Security modes
- c. Biba Model
- d. Lattice-based access control

Guidance: level 1

:: Computer security ::

_____ are safeguards or countermeasures to avoid, detect, counteract, or minimize security risks to physical property, information, computer systems, or other assets.

Exam Probability: **Medium**

48. *Answer choices:*
(see index for correct answer)

- a. Ambient authority
- b. Federal Information Security Management Act of 2002
- c. Event Management
- d. Cyber spying

Guidance: level 1

:: Cryptography ::

The Secure Hash Algorithms are a family of cryptographic hash functions published by the National Institute of Standards and Technology as a U.S. Federal Information Processing Standard , including.

Exam Probability: **Low**

49. *Answer choices:*

(see index for correct answer)

- a. Discrete logarithm
- b. Secure Hash Standard
- c. SPKAC
- d. Proxy re-encryption

Guidance: level 1

:: Electronic documents ::

A _____ is a mathematical scheme for verifying the authenticity of digital messages or documents. A valid _____ , where the prerequisites are satisfied, gives a recipient very strong reason to believe that the message was created by a known sender , and that the message was not altered in transit .

Exam Probability: **High**

50. *Answer choices:*

(see index for correct answer)

- a. Digital signature
- b. Electronic article
- c. Archival Resource Key
- d. SAFE-BioPharma Association

:: Computing platforms ::

_____ is a family of open source Unix-like operating systems based on the _____ kernel, an operating system kernel first released on September 17, 1991 by Linus Torvalds. _____ is typically packaged in a _____ distribution .

Exam Probability: **High**

51. *Answer choices:*

(see index for correct answer)

- a. Linux
- b. Mono
- c. ClickOnce
- d. Sigar

:: Domain name system ::

Within the Internet, _____ s are formed by the rules and procedures of the _____ System. Any name registered in the DNS is a _____. _____ s are used in various networking contexts and for application-specific naming and addressing purposes. In general, a _____ represents an Internet Protocol resource, such as a personal computer used to access the Internet, a server computer hosting a web site, or the web site itself or any other service communicated via the Internet. In 2017, 330.6 million _____ s had been registered.

Exam Probability: **High**

52. *Answer choices:*

(see index for correct answer)

- a. Domain name front running
- b. Reverse DNS lookup
- c. Domain name
- d. DNS blocking

Guidance: level 1

:: Application layer protocols ::

The _____ is a network management protocol used on UDP/IP networks whereby a DHCP server dynamically assigns an IP address and other network configuration parameters to each device on a network so they can communicate with other IP networks. A DHCP server enables computers to request IP addresses and networking parameters automatically from the Internet service provider, reducing the need for a network administrator or a user to manually assign IP addresses to all network devices. In the absence of a DHCP server, a computer or other device on the network needs to be manually assigned an IP address, or to assign itself an APIPA address, which will not enable it to communicate outside its local subnet.

Exam Probability: **Low**

53. *Answer choices:*

(see index for correct answer)

- a. Dynamic Host Configuration Protocol
- b. Java Naming and Directory Interface
- c. NETCONF
- d. Etch

Guidance: level 1

:: Cryptographic attacks ::

In cryptanalysis and computer security, a _____ is a form of brute force attack technique for defeating a cipher or authentication mechanism by trying to determine its decryption key or passphrase by trying hundreds or sometimes millions of likely possibilities, such as words in a dictionary.

54. *Answer choices:*

(see index for correct answer)

- a. Keystroke logging
- b. Attack model
- c. Custom hardware attack
- d. Dictionary attack

Guidance: level 1

:: Computer networking ::

In the seven-layer OSI model of computer networking, the _____ or layer 1 is the first and lowest layer. This layer may be implemented by a PHY chip.

Exam Probability: **Medium**

55. *Answer choices:*

(see index for correct answer)

- a. Physical layer
- b. Synchronous virtual pipe
- c. Network forensics
- d. Multimedia over Coax Alliance

:: Computer security ::

In information security, computer science, and other fields, the principle of _____ , also known as the principle of minimal privilege or the principle of least authority, requires that in a particular abstraction layer of a computing environment, every module must be able to access only the information and resources that are necessary for its legitimate purpose.

Exam Probability: **Medium**

56. *Answer choices:*

(see index for correct answer)

- a. Least privilege
- b. Proof-carrying code
- c. Cyber Storm Exercise
- d. Federal Information Security Management Act of 2002

:: Searches and seizures ::

A _____ is a court order that a magistrate or judge issues to authorize law enforcement officers to conduct a search of a person, location, or vehicle for evidence of a crime and to confiscate any evidence they find. In most countries, a _____ cannot be issued in aid of civil process.

Exam Probability: **Medium**

57. *Answer choices:*

(see index for correct answer)

- a. Frisking
- b. Search warrant
- c. Knock-and-announce
- d. Body cavity search

Guidance: level 1

:: Computer security exploits ::

In computer security, a _____ is a type of attack that creates a capability to transfer information objects between processes that are not supposed to be allowed to communicate by the computer security policy. The term, originated in 1973 by Lampson, is defined as channels "not intended for information transfer at all, such as the service program's effect on system load," to distinguish it from legitimate channels that are subjected to access controls by COMPUSEC.

Exam Probability: **Low**

58. *Answer choices:*

(see index for correct answer)

- a. Shoulder surfing
- b. Covert channel
- c. GetAdmin
- d. Session hijacking

Guidance: level 1

:: Internet protocols ::

_____ is an Internet protocol that exchanges network packets between a client and server through a proxy server. _____ 5 additionally provides authentication so only authorized users may access a server. Practically, a _____ server proxies TCP connections to an arbitrary IP address, and provides a means for UDP packets to be forwarded.

Exam Probability: **Medium**

59. *Answer choices:*

(see index for correct answer)

- a. Port
- b. MS-CHAP
- c. Bridging Systems Interface
- d. Common Open Policy Service

Guidance: level 1

Theoretical computer science

Theoretical computer science is a subset of general computer science and mathematics that focuses on more mathematical topics of computing and includes the theory of computation. While logical it is inference and mathematical proof had existed previously, in 1931 Kurt Gödel proved with his incompleteness theorem that there are fundamental limitations on what statements could be proved or disproved. These developments have led to the modern study of logic and computability, and indeed the field of theoretical computer science as a whole

:: Information theory ::

_____ of signal is defined as the deliberate process of expanding the frequency range of a signal in which it contains an appreciable and useful content, and/or the frequency range in which its effects are such. Its significant advancement in recent years has led to the technology being adopted commercially in several areas including psychacoustic bass enhancement of small loudspeakers and the high frequency enhancement of coded speech and audio.

Exam Probability: **High**

1. *Answer choices:*

(see index for correct answer)

- a. Bandwidth extension
- b. Surprisal Analysis
- c. Water-pouring algorithm
- d. Kolmogorov complexity

Guidance: level 1

:: Computational science ::

_____ refers to the methods and computing tools developed in and used by particle physics research. Like computational chemistry or computational biology, it is, for particle physics both a specific branch and an interdisciplinary field relying on computer science, theoretical and experimental particle physics and mathematics. The main fields of _____ are: lattice field theory , automatic calculation of particle interaction or decay and event generators .

Exam Probability: **High**

2. *Answer choices:*

(see index for correct answer)

- a. Computational particle physics
- b. NanoLanguage
- c. Atomistix Virtual NanoLab
- d. Computational topology

Guidance: level 1

:: Data types ::

_____ is a relation between objects in which one object designates, or acts as a means by which to connect to or link to, another object. The first object in this relation is said to refer to the second object. It is called a name for the second object. The second object, the one to which the first object refers, is called the referent of the first object. A name is usually a phrase or expression, or some other symbolic representation. Its referent may be anything – a material object, a person, an event, an activity, or an abstract concept.

Exam Probability: **Low**

3. *Answer choices:*

(see index for correct answer)

- a. Anonymous type
- b. Polymorphism
- c. Reference
- d. Type class

Guidance: level 1

:: Formal methods ::

A _____ is a generalization of the binary decision diagram to linear functions over domains such as booleans , but also to integers or to real numbers.

Exam Probability: **Medium**

4. *Answer choices:*

- a. Algebraic semantics
- b. Language Of Temporal Ordering Specification
- c. And-inverter graph
- d. Construction and Analysis of Distributed Processes

Guidance: level 1

:: Virtual reality ::

_____ is the reproduction of the behavior of a system using a computer to simulate the outcomes of a mathematical model associated with said system. Since they allow to check the reliability of chosen mathematical models, _____ s have become a useful tool for the mathematical modeling of many natural systems in physics , astrophysics, climatology, chemistry, biology and manufacturing, human systems in economics, psychology, social science, health care and engineering. Simulation of a system is represented as the running of the system's model. It can be used to explore and gain new insights into new technology and to estimate the performance of systems too complex for analytical solutions.

Exam Probability: **Low**

5. *Answer choices:*

- a. XVROS

- b. Computer simulation
- c. Transformed social interaction
- d. Rumble Pak

Guidance: level 1

:: Numerical analysis ::

In botany, _____ s are the flowers of stone fruit trees and of some other plants with a similar appearance that flower profusely for a period of time in spring.

Exam Probability: **High**

6. *Answer choices:*

(see index for correct answer)

- a. Blossom
- b. Bernstein polynomial
- c. Boundary knot method
- d. Numerical continuation

Guidance: level 1

:: Cryptography ::

_____ is a cryptographic tool, introduced by Stephen Wiesner in the late 1960s. It is part of the two applications Wiesner described for quantum coding, along with a method for creating fraud-proof banking notes. The application where the concept was based from was a method of transmitting multiple messages in such a way that reading one destroys the others. This is called quantum multiplexing and it uses photons polarized in conjugate bases as "qubits" to pass information. _____ also is a simple extension of a random number generator.

Exam Probability: **Medium**

7. *Answer choices:*

(see index for correct answer)

- a. Texas Instruments signing key controversy
- b. Password-based cryptography
- c. Conjugate coding
- d. Key number method

Guidance: level 1

:: Natural language processing ::

A _____ is a description of how two segments of discourse are logically connected to one another.

Exam Probability: **Low**

8. *Answer choices:*

(see index for correct answer)

- a. Robby Garner
- b. Discourse relation
- c. Open domain question answering
- d. PropBank

Guidance: level 1

:: Artificial intelligence ::

In artificial intelligence, an _____ is a computer system that emulates the decision-making ability of a human expert. _____ s are designed to solve complex problems by reasoning through bodies of knowledge, represented mainly as if–then rules rather than through conventional procedural code. The first _____ s were created in the 1970s and then proliferated in the 1980s. _____ s were among the first truly successful forms of artificial intelligence software. However, some experts point out that _____ s were not part of true artificial intelligence since they lack the ability to learn autonomously from external data. An _____ is divided into two subsystems: the inference engine and the knowledge base. The knowledge base represents facts and rules. The inference engine applies the rules to the known facts to deduce new facts. Inference engines can also include explanation and debugging abilities.

Exam Probability: **Low**

9. *Answer choices:*

(see index for correct answer)

- a. Intelligent decision support systems
- b. Philosophy of Artificial Intelligence and Cognitive Science
- c. Psychology of reasoning
- d. Expert system

Guidance: level 1

:: Numerical analysis ::

In mathematics, a _____ is a numerical analysis technique used in computer simulation for solving ordinary differential equations by converting them to hyperbolic equations. In this way an explicit solution scheme is obtained with highly robust numerical properties. It was introduced by Auslander in 1968.

Exam Probability: **Medium**

10. *Answer choices:*
(see index for correct answer)

- a. Newton fractal
- b. G space
- c. Blossom
- d. Trajectory

Guidance: level 1

:: Static program analysis tools ::

_____ is a computer software tool designed to find possible coding faults in the Linux kernel. Unlike other such tools, this static analysis tool was initially designed to only flag constructs that were likely to be of interest to kernel developers, such as the mixing of pointers to user and kernel address spaces.

Exam Probability: **High**

11. *Answer choices:*

(see index for correct answer)

- a. Fortify Software
- b. PerlTidy
- c. AbsInt
- d. Sparse

Guidance: level 1

:: Formal methods ::

In the context of hardware and software systems, _____ is the act of proving or disproving the correctness of intended algorithms underlying a system with respect to a certain formal specification or property, using formal methods of mathematics.

12. *Answer choices:*

(see index for correct answer)

- a. Lambda calculus
- b. Statistical static timing analysis
- c. Set theory
- d. Formal verification

Guidance: level 1

:: Numerical analysis ::

In mathematics, the _____ , named after the New Zealand mathematician John C. Butcher by , is an infinite-dimensional Lie group first introduced in numerical analysis to study solutions of non-linear ordinary differential equations by the RungeKutta method. It arose from an algebraic formalism involving rooted trees that provides formal power series solutions of the differential equation modeling the flow of a vector field. It was , prompted by the work of Sylvester on change of variables in differential calculus, who first noted that the derivatives of a composition of functions can be conveniently expressed in terms of rooted trees and their combinatorics.

Exam Probability: **Medium**

13. *Answer choices:*

(see index for correct answer)

- a. Butcher group
- b. Sparse grid
- c. Singular boundary method
- d. Rigorous coupled-wave analysis

Guidance: level 1

:: Sequences and series ::

In statistics, _____ s are sequences used to generate points in space for numerical methods such as Monte Carlo simulations. Although these sequences are deterministic, they are of low discrepancy, that is, appear to be random for many purposes. They were first introduced in 1960 and are an example of a quasi-random number sequence. They generalise the one-dimensional van der Corput sequences.

Exam Probability: **High**

14. *Answer choices:*

(see index for correct answer)

- a. Shift rule
- b. Spread polynomials
- c. Periodic sequence
- d. Sturmian word

Guidance: level 1

:: Control characters ::

_____ is the boundless three-dimensional extent in which objects and events have relative position and direction. Physical _____ is often conceived in three linear dimensions, although modern physicists usually consider it, with time, to be part of a boundless four-dimensional continuum known as _____ time. The concept of _____ is considered to be of fundamental importance to an understanding of the physical universe. However, disagreement continues between philosophers over whether it is itself an entity, a relationship between entities, or part of a conceptual framework.

Exam Probability: **Medium**

15. *Answer choices:*

(see index for correct answer)

- a. Eight Ones
- b. End-of-transmission character
- c. Left-to-right mark
- d. Space

Guidance: level 1

:: Automata theory ::

In the theory of computation, a branch of theoretical computer science, a _____ is a type of automaton that employs a stack.

16. *Answer choices:*

(see index for correct answer)

- a. Augmented transition network
- b. Pushdown automaton
- c. Two-way deterministic finite automaton
- d. Recognizable set

Guidance: level 1

:: Artificial life ::

_____ is a 1983 novel by British science fiction author James P. Hogan. NASA's Advanced Automation for Space Missions was the direct inspiration for this novel detailing first contact between Earth explorers and the Taloids, clanking replicators who have colonized Saturn's moon Titan.

Exam Probability: **Low**

17. *Answer choices:*

(see index for correct answer)

- a. Code of the Lifemaker
- b. Clanking replicator
- c. Evolving digital ecological networks

- d. Creatures 2

Guidance: level 1

:: Logic in computer science ::

_____ is a variety of substructural logic proposed by Peter O`Hearn and David Pym. _____ provides primitives for reasoning about resource composition, which aid in the compositional analysis of computer and other systems. It has category-theoretic and truth-functional semantics which can be understood in terms of an abstract concept of resource, and a proof theory in which the contexts G in an entailment judgement G A are tree-like structures rather than lists or sets as in most proof calculi. _____ has an associated type theory, and its first application was in providing a way to control the aliasing and other forms of interference in imperative programs. The logic has seen further applications in program verification, where it is the basis of the assertion language of separation logic, and in systems modelling, where it provides a way to decompose the resources used by components of a system.

Exam Probability: **Low**

18. *Answer choices:*
(see index for correct answer)

- a. Forward chaining
- b. Combinational logic
- c. Twelf
- d. Bunched logic

:: Wavelets ::

In numerical analysis and functional analysis, a _____ is any wavelet transform for which the wavelets are discretely sampled. As with other wavelet transforms, a key advantage it has over Fourier transforms is temporal resolution: it captures both frequency and location information .

Exam Probability: **High**

19. *Answer choices:*

(see index for correct answer)

- a. Multiresolution analysis
- b. Multigrid method
- c. Discrete wavelet transform
- d. Dynamic link matching

:: Root-finding algorithms ::

In mathematics and computing, a _____ is an algorithm for finding roots of continuous functions. A root of a function f, from the real numbers to real numbers or from the complex numbers to the complex numbers, is a number x such that f = 0. As, generally, the roots of a function cannot be computed exactly, nor expressed in closed form, _____ s provide approximations to roots, expressed either as floating point numbers or as small isolating intervals, or disks for complex roots .

Exam Probability: **Low**

20. *Answer choices:*

(see index for correct answer)

- a. Root-finding algorithm
- b. Fixed-point iteration
- c. Rational root theorem
- d. Splitting circle method

Guidance: level 1

:: Computational science ::

_____ is a term used in a variety of projects involved in making access to bioinformatics software on a Linux platform easier using one or more of the following methods.

Exam Probability: **Medium**

21. *Answer choices:*

(see index for correct answer)

- a. OLGA
- b. BioLinux
- c. OpenFOAM
- d. Transmission-line matrix method

Guidance: level 1

:: Theory of computation ::

In physics and cosmology, _____ is a collection of theoretical perspectives based on the premise that the universe is describable by information. It is a form of digital ontology about the physical reality. According to this theory, the universe can be conceived of as either the output of a deterministic or probabilistic computer program, a vast, digital computation device, or mathematically isomorphic to such a device.

Exam Probability: **Low**

22. *Answer choices:*

(see index for correct answer)

- a. Reachability problem
- b. Theory of computation
- c. Description number
- d. Self-reference

:: Artificial life ::

The field bears some similarity to artificial life, but unlike artificial life, _____ focuses on the primary emergence of complex structures and processes of abiogenesis. _____ does not rely exclusively on the application of evolutionary computation and genetic algorithms to optimize artificial creatures or grow synthetic life forms. _____ instead studies systems of rules of interaction, initial conditions and primordial building blocks that can generate complex lifelike structures, based exclusively on repeated application of rules of interaction.

Exam Probability: **Medium**

23. *Answer choices:*

(see index for correct answer)

- a. Artificial creation
- b. Self-replication
- c. Boids
- d. Creatures 3

:: Automata theory ::

In computer science, a _____ is a concept of automata theory in which the outcome of a transition from one state to another is determined by the input.

Exam Probability: **High**

24. *Answer choices:*

(see index for correct answer)

- a. Powerset construction
- b. Cellular automaton
- c. Tree automaton
- d. Star height problem

Guidance: level 1

:: Artificial life ::

An _____ is a chemical-like system that usually consists of objects, called molecules, that interact according to rules resembling chemical reaction rules. Artificial chemistries are created and studied in order to understand fundamental properties of chemical systems, including prebiotic evolution, as well as for developing chemical computing systems. _____ is a field within computer science wherein chemical reactions—often biochemical ones—are computer-simulated, yielding insights on evolution, self-assembly, and other biochemical phenomena. The field does not use actual chemicals, and should not be confused with either synthetic chemistry or computational chemistry. Rather, bits of information are used to represent the starting molecules, and the end products are examined along with the processes that led to them. The field originated in artificial life but has shown to be a versatile method with applications in many fields such as chemistry, economics, sociology and linguistics.

Exam Probability: **Medium**

25. *Answer choices:*

(see index for correct answer)

- a. Creatures 2
- b. Artificially Expanded Genetic Information System
- c. Synthetic Organism Designer
- d. Artificial chemistry

Guidance: level 1

:: Information theory ::

In information theory, the _____ is a general property of the output samples of a stochastic source. It is fundamental to the concept of typical set used in theories of compression.

Exam Probability: **Medium**

26. *Answer choices:*

(see index for correct answer)

- a. Grammar-based code
- b. Specific-information
- c. Information source
- d. Triangular network coding

Guidance: level 1

:: Bioinformatics software ::

_____ is a free online bioinformatics resource developed by the Laboratory of Immunopathogenesis and Bioinformatics . All tools in the _____ Bioinformatics Resources aim to provide functional interpretation of large lists of genes derived from genomic studies, e.g. microarray and proteomics studies. _____ can be found at http:// _____ .niaid.nih.gov or http:// _____ .abcc.ncifcrf.gov

Exam Probability: **Low**

27. *Answer choices:*

- a. DAVID
- b. GENSCAN
- c. Clustal
- d. Vector NTI

Guidance: level 1

:: Theoretical computer science conferences ::

The _____ is the premier academic _____ and related fields. The first CADE was organized in 1974 at the Argonne National Laboratory near Chicago. Most CADE meetings have been held in Europe and the United States. However, conferences have been held all over the world. Since 1996, CADE has been held yearly. In 2001, CADE was, for the first time, merged into the International Joint Conference on Automated Reasoning . This has been repeated biannually since 2004.

Exam Probability: **Medium**

28. *Answer choices:*

- a. International Conference on Theory and Applications of Models of Computation
- b. Algorithmic Number Theory Symposium

- c. Symposium on Theory of Computing
- d. Symposium on Foundations of Computer Science

Guidance: level 1

:: Genetic algorithms ::

_____ is a Microsoft Windows compatibility layer available for Linux, macOS, and Chrome OS. This compatibility layer enables many Windows-based applications to run on Linux operating systems, macOS, or Chrome OS.

Exam Probability: **Medium**

29. *Answer choices:*

(see index for correct answer)

- a. Truncation selection
- b. Quality control and genetic algorithms
- c. Genetic fuzzy systems
- d. CrossOver

Guidance: level 1

:: Automata theory ::

A _____ is a system with a countable number of states. _____ s may be contrasted with continuous systems, which may also be called analog systems. A final _____ is often modeled with a directed graph and is analyzed for correctness and complexity according to computational theory. Because _____ s have a countable number of states, they may be described in precise mathematical models.

Exam Probability: **Medium**

30. *Answer choices:*

(see index for correct answer)

- a. Queue automaton
- b. Discrete system
- c. Pumping lemma for regular languages
- d. Abstract machine

Guidance: level 1

:: Compilers ::

A _____ is a computer program that translates computer code written in one programming language into another programming language . The name _____ is primarily used for programs that translate source code from a high-level programming language to a lower level language to create an executable program.

Exam Probability: **Medium**

31. *Answer choices:*

(see index for correct answer)

- a. The Design of an Optimizing Compiler
- b. Laning and Zierler system
- c. Vector Fabrics, B.V.
- d. Red zone

Guidance: level 1

:: Computational science ::

_____ is a rapidly growing multidisciplinary field that uses advanced computing capabilities to understand and solve complex problems. It is an area of science which spans many disciplines, but at its core it involves the development of models and simulations to understand natural systems.

Exam Probability: **Low**

32. *Answer choices:*

(see index for correct answer)

- a. Numerical analysis
- b. Computational criminology
- c. Computational epidemiology
- d. European Conference on Computational Biology

:: Theoretical computer science ::

The _____ is an organisation, founded in 1985, that represents the interests of Theoretical Computer Science in the UK, e.g. through representation on academic boards and providing commentary and evidence in response to consultations from public bodies. The BCTCS operates under the direction of an Organising Committee, with an Executive consisting of a President, Secretary and Treasurer. The current President is Barnaby Martin.

Exam Probability: **Low**

33. *Answer choices:*

(see index for correct answer)

- a. British Colloquium for Theoretical Computer Science
- b. Fredkin finite nature hypothesis
- c. LogP machine
- d. Bio-inspired computing

:: Computational science ::

_____ is a broad field that attempts to optimize societal, economic, and environmental resources using methods from mathematics and computer science fields. Sustainability in this context is the ability to produce enough energy for the world to support its biological systems. Using the power of computers to process large quantities of information, decision making algorithms allocate resources based on real-time information.

Exam Probability: **High**

34. *Answer choices:*

(see index for correct answer)

- a. Computational Sustainability
- b. EPCC
- c. Information visualization reference model
- d. Computer experiment

Guidance: level 1

:: Numerical analysis ::

In mathematics, _____ is concerned with how functions can best be approximated with simpler functions, and with quantitatively characterizing the errors introduced thereby. Note that what is meant by best and simpler will depend on the application.

Exam Probability: **High**

35. *Answer choices:*

- a. Approximation theory
- b. Adjoint state method
- c. Method of fundamental solutions
- d. Numerical stability

Guidance: level 1

:: Theoretical computer science ::

In mathematics, computer science, and linguistics, a _____ consists of words whose letters are taken from an alphabet and are well-formed according to a specific set of rules.

Exam Probability: **High**

36. *Answer choices:*

- a. Computational learning theory
- b. Formal language
- c. DNA computing
- d. Indirect self-reference

Guidance: level 1

:: Computational complexity theory ::

_____ s in computational complexity theory are problems stated in terms of the changing input data. In the most general form a problem in this category is usually stated as follows.

Exam Probability: **High**

37. *Answer choices:*

(see index for correct answer)

- a. Truth-table reduction
- b. Leaf language
- c. Complexity class
- d. Dynamic problem

Guidance: level 1

:: Digital signal processing ::

In a mixed-signal system , a _____ is used to construct a smooth analog signal from a digital input, as in the case of a digital to analog converter or other sampled data output device.

Exam Probability: **Low**

38. *Answer choices:*

(see index for correct answer)

- a. Bilinear transform
- b. Nyquist frequency
- c. Reconstruction filter
- d. Geometric Arithmetic Parallel Processor

Guidance: level 1

:: Machine learning ::

The _____ refers to various phenomena that arise when analyzing and organizing data in high-dimensional spaces that do not occur in low-dimensional settings such as the three-dimensional physical space of everyday experience. The expression was coined by Richard E. Bellman when considering problems in dynamic optimization.

Exam Probability: **High**

39. *Answer choices:*

(see index for correct answer)

- a. PU learning
- b. Curse of dimensionality
- c. Active learning
- d. Elastic matching

:: Computational science ::

_____ is a component based scientific computing environment that handles high-performance computing problems with focus on complex computational fluid dynamics involving multiphysics phenomena.

Exam Probability: **High**

40. *Answer choices:*

(see index for correct answer)

- a. Computational chemical methods in solid-state physics
- b. Computational steering
- c. BioSim
- d. Muffin-tin approximation

:: Pseudoscience ::

In physics, _____ is the quantitative property that must be transferred to an object in order to perform work on, or to heat, the object. _____ is a conserved quantity; the law of conservation of _____ states that _____ can be converted in form, but not created or destroyed. The SI unit of _____ is the joule, which is the _____ transferred to an object by the work of moving it a distance of 1 metre against a force of 1 newton.

Exam Probability: **Low**

41. *Answer choices:*

(see index for correct answer)

- a. Hindu astrology
- b. Toftness device
- c. Energy
- d. Flood geology

Guidance: level 1

:: Wavelets ::

A _____ is a wave-like oscillation with an amplitude that begins at zero, increases, and then decreases back to zero. It can typically be visualized as a "brief oscillation" like one recorded by a seismograph or heart monitor. Generally, _____ s are intentionally crafted to have specific properties that make them useful for signal processing. Using a "reverse, shift, multiply and integrate" technique called convolution, _____ s can be combined with known portions of a damaged signal to extract information from the unknown portions.

42. *Answer choices:*

(see index for correct answer)

- a. Fast wavelet transform
- b. Bandelet
- c. Wavelet
- d. Lifting scheme

Guidance: level 1

:: Graph theory ::

In mathematics, the _____ is an analog of the continuous Laplace operator, defined so that it has meaning on a graph or a discrete grid. For the case of a finite-dimensional graph , the _____ is more commonly called the Laplacian matrix.

Exam Probability: **Medium**

43. *Answer choices:*

(see index for correct answer)

- a. Shortest-path tree
- b. Interval
- c. Resistance distance

- d. Discrete Laplace operator

Guidance: level 1

:: Theory of computation ::

In computability theory a _____ is a construction that associates a cylindric numbering to each numbering. The concept was first introduced by Yuri L. Ershov in 1973.

Exam Probability: **Medium**

44. *Answer choices:*

(see index for correct answer)

- a. Wang tile
- b. Simply typed lambda calculus
- c. Hypercomputation
- d. Cylindrification

Guidance: level 1

:: Data types ::

In linguistics, a _____ is the smallest element that can be uttered in isolation with objective or practical meaning.

Exam Probability: **Medium**

45. *Answer choices:*

(see index for correct answer)

- a. Word
- b. Integer
- c. Pointer
- d. Real data type

Guidance: level 1

:: Probability distributions ::

In probability theory and statistics, a _____ is a mathematical function that provides the probabilities of occurrence of different possible outcomes in an experiment. In more technical terms, the _____ is a description of a random phenomenon in terms of the probabilities of events. For instance, if the random variable X is used to denote the outcome of a coin toss , then the _____ of X would take the value 0.5 for X = heads, and 0.5 for X = tails . Examples of random phenomena can include the results of an experiment or survey.

Exam Probability: **High**

46. *Answer choices:*

(see index for correct answer)

- a. Crystal Ball function
- b. Mittag-leffler distribution
- c. Consumption distribution
- d. Null distribution

Guidance: level 1

:: Numerical analysis ::

_____ is a model for self-validated numerical analysis. In AA, the quantities of interest are represented as affine combinations of certain primitive variables, which stand for sources of uncertainty in the data or approximations made during the computation.

Exam Probability: **Low**

47. *Answer choices:*

(see index for correct answer)

- a. Sinc numerical methods
- b. Rate of convergence
- c. Successive parabolic interpolation
- d. Finite-volume method

:: Computational science ::

_____ , formerly the Edinburgh Parallel Computing Centre, is a supercomputing centre based at the University of Edinburgh. Since its foundation in 1990, its stated mission has been to accelerate the effective exploitation of novel computing throughout industry, academia and commerce.

Exam Probability: **High**

48. *Answer choices:*

(see index for correct answer)

- a. Muffin-tin approximation
- b. EPCC
- c. Vis5D
- d. MacVector

:: Evolutionary computation ::

_____ is an evolutionary reinforcement learning method that evolves both the topology and weights of artificial neural networks. It is closely related to the works of Angeline et al. and Stanley and Miikkulainen. Like the work of Angeline et al., the method uses a type of parametric mutation that comes from evolution strategies and evolutionary programming , in which adaptive step sizes are used for optimizing the weights of the neural networks. Similar to the work of Stanley , the method starts with minimal structures which gain complexity along the evolution path.

Exam Probability: **High**

49. *Answer choices:*

(see index for correct answer)

- a. IEEE Congress on Evolutionary Computation
- b. Cooperative coevolution
- c. DEAP
- d. Evolutionary Acquisition of Neural Topologies

Guidance: level 1

:: Neural networks ::

In artificial neural networks, the _____ of a node defines the output of that node, or "neuron," given an input or set of inputs. This output is then used as input for the next node and so on until a desired solution to the original problem is found.

50. *Answer choices:*

(see index for correct answer)

- a. Probabilistic neural network
- b. Long short term memory
- c. Activation function
- d. Biological neural network

Guidance: level 1

:: Real analysis ::

In mathematics, the _____ , discovered by Henry Wilbraham and rediscovered by J. Willard Gibbs , is the peculiar manner in which the Fourier series of a piecewise continuously differentiable periodic function behaves at a jump discontinuity. The nth partial sum of the Fourier series has large oscillations near the jump, which might increase the maximum of the partial sum above that of the function itself. The overshoot does not die out as n increases, but approaches a finite limit. This sort of behavior was also observed by experimental physicists, but was believed to be due to imperfections in the measuring apparatuses.

Exam Probability: **Medium**

51. *Answer choices:*

(see index for correct answer)

- a. Gibbs phenomenon
- b. Semi-differentiability
- c. Invex function
- d. Piecewise linear function

Guidance: level 1

:: Formal languages ::

In formal language theory, weak equivalence of two grammars means they generate the same set of strings, i.e. that the formal language they generate is the same. In compiler theory the notion is distinguished from strong equivalence, which additionally means that the two parse trees are reasonably similar in that the same semantic interpretation can be assigned to both.

Exam Probability: **Low**

52. *Answer choices:*
(see index for correct answer)

- a. Weak generative capacity
- b. LR-attributed grammar
- c. Free monoid
- d. Context-sensitive language

Guidance: level 1

:: Information theory ::

In radio, multiple-input and multiple-output, or _____ , is a method for multiplying the capacity of a radio link using multiple transmission and receiving antennas to exploit multipath propagation. _____ has become an essential element of wireless communication standards including IEEE 802.11n , IEEE 802.11ac , HSPA+ , WiMAX , and Long Term Evolution . More recently, _____ has been applied to power-line communication for 3-wire installations as part of ITU G.hn standard and HomePlug AV2 specification.

Exam Probability: **Low**

53. *Answer choices:*

(see index for correct answer)

- a. MIMO
- b. The Three-Process View
- c. Z-channel
- d. Code rate

Guidance: level 1

:: Computational science ::

The _____ , is a mathematical tool for reconstructing a volume-covering and continuous density or intensity field from a discrete point set. The DTFE has various astrophysical applications, such as the analysis of numerical simulations of cosmic structure formation, the mapping of the large-scale structure of the universe and improving computer simulation programs of cosmic structure formation. It has been developed by Willem Schaap and Rien van de Weijgaert. The main advantage of the DTFE is that it automatically adapts to variations in density and geometry. It is therefore very well suited for studies of the large scale galaxy distribution.

Exam Probability: **High**

54. *Answer choices:*

(see index for correct answer)

- a. Beam propagation method
- b. Computational scientist
- c. Intracule
- d. VisAD

Guidance: level 1

:: Formal methods ::

In computer science and mathematical logic, a proof assistant or interactive theorem prover is a software tool to assist with the development of formal proofs by human-machine collaboration. This involves some sort of interactive proof editor, or other interface, with which a human can guide the search for proofs, the details of which are stored in, and some steps provided by, a computer.

Exam Probability: **Low**

55. *Answer choices:*

(see index for correct answer)

- a. Oracle Unified Method
- b. Verification and validation
- c. Assertion
- d. Automated proof checking

Guidance: level 1

:: Formal languages ::

An _____ is a grouping of generalized acceptors. Informally, an acceptor is a device with a finite state control, a finite number of input symbols, and an internal store with a read and write function. Each acceptor has a start state and a set of accepting states. The device reads a sequence of symbols, transitioning from state to state for each input symbol. If the device ends in an accepting state, the device is said to accept the sequence of symbols. A family of acceptors is a set of acceptors with the same type of internal store. The study of AFA is part of AFL theory.

56. *Answer choices:*

(see index for correct answer)

- a. Recursive grammar
- b. Straight-line grammar
- c. Erasing rule
- d. Abstract family of acceptors

Guidance: level 1

:: Mathematics of computing ::

In mathematics, _____ is the study of the way general functions may be represented or approximated by sums of simpler trigonometric functions.
_____ grew from the study of Fourier series, and is named after Joseph Fourier, who showed that representing a function as a sum of trigonometric functions greatly simplifies the study of heat transfer.

Exam Probability: **High**

57. *Answer choices:*

(see index for correct answer)

- a. Fixed-point combinator
- b. Fourier analysis

- c. Log probability

Guidance: level 1

:: Fractals ::

_____ is the repetition of a process in order to generate a sequence of outcomes. The sequence will approach some end point or end value. Each repetition of the process is a single _____ , and the outcome of each _____ is then the starting point of the next _____ .

Exam Probability: **Medium**

58. *Answer choices:*

(see index for correct answer)

- a. Mandelbrot set
- b. Iteration
- c. Minkowski content
- d. Singularity spectrum

Guidance: level 1

:: Fourier analysis ::

In mathematics, the _____ is an integral transform named after its inventor Pierre-Simon Laplace . It takes a function of a real variable t to a function of a complex variable s . The transform has many applications in science and engineering.

Exam Probability: **Low**

59. *Answer choices:*

(see index for correct answer)

- a. Laplace transform
- b. Homogeneous distribution
- c. Fourier transform
- d. Bragg plane

Guidance: level 1

Information technology

Information technology is the use of computers to store, retrieve, transmit, and manipulate data, or information, often in the context of a business or other enterprise. IT is considered to be a subset of information and communications technology.

:: Photo software ::

_____ was an augmented reality translation application from Quest Visual. _____ used the built-in cameras on smartphones and similar devices to quickly scan and identify foreign text , and then translate and display the words in another language on the device`s display. The words were displayed in the original context on the original background, and the translation was performed in real-time without connection to the internet. For example, using the viewfinder of a camera to show a shop sign on a smartphone`s display would result in a real-time image of the shop sign being displayed, but the words shown on the sign would be the translated words instead of the original foreign words.

Exam Probability: **Medium**

1. *Answer choices:*

(see index for correct answer)

- a. Process
- b. Serif PhotoPlus
- c. Word Lens
- d. Capture NX

Guidance: level 1

:: Virtual economy ::

_____ is an online virtual world, developed and owned by the San Francisco-based firm Linden Lab and launched on June 23, 2003. By 2013, _____ had approximately one million regular users; at the end of 2017 active user count totals "between 800,000 and 900,000". In many ways, _____ is similar to massively multiplayer online role-playing games; however, Linden Lab is emphatic that their creation is not a game: "There is no manufactured conflict, no set objective".

Exam Probability: **High**

2. *Answer choices:*

(see index for correct answer)

- a. Second Life
- b. Frontier: Elite II
- c. Red Butler
- d. Blue Mars

Guidance: level 1

:: Abstraction ::

_____ is the state or quality of being simple. Something easy to understand or explain seems simple, in contrast to something complicated. Alternatively, as Herbert A. Simon suggests, something is simple or complex depending on the way we choose to describe it. In some uses, the label " _____ " can imply beauty, purity, or clarity. In other cases, the term may occur with negative connotations to suggest, a deficit or insufficiency of nuance or of complexity of a thing, relative to what one supposes as required.

3. *Answer choices:*

(see index for correct answer)

- a. Simplicity
- b. Abstractionism
- c. Object of the mind
- d. Abstract structure

Guidance: level 1

:: Database management systems ::

A _____ is a digital database based on the relational model of data, as proposed by E. F. Codd in 1970. A software system used to maintain _____ s is a _____ management system . Virtually all _____ systems use SQL for querying and maintaining the database.

Exam Probability: **Medium**

4. *Answer choices:*

(see index for correct answer)

- a. Secondary database server
- b. Correlation database
- c. Vectorwise

- d. Data control language

Guidance: level 1

:: Scientific method ::

In the social sciences and life sciences, a _____ is a research method involving an up-close, in-depth, and detailed examination of a subject of study , as well as its related contextual conditions.

Exam Probability: **Low**

5. *Answer choices:*

(see index for correct answer)

- a. Cybermethodology
- b. Interdisciplinary peer review
- c. Woozle effect
- d. Free parameter

Guidance: level 1

:: Control characters ::

_____ is the boundless three-dimensional extent in which objects and events have relative position and direction. Physical _____ is often conceived in three linear dimensions, although modern physicists usually consider it, with time, to be part of a boundless four-dimensional continuum known as _____ time. The concept of _____ is considered to be of fundamental importance to an understanding of the physical universe. However, disagreement continues between philosophers over whether it is itself an entity, a relationship between entities, or part of a conceptual framework.

Exam Probability: **Medium**

6. *Answer choices:*

(see index for correct answer)

- a. Non-breaking space
- b. Space
- c. Line starve
- d. Zero-width joiner

Guidance: level 1

:: E-commerce ::

The phrase _____ was originally coined in 1997 by Kevin Duffey at the launch of the Global _____ Forum, to mean "the delivery of electronic commerce capabilities directly into the consumer's hand, anywhere, via wireless technology." Many choose to think of _____ as meaning "a retail outlet in your customer's pocket."

7. *Answer choices:*

(see index for correct answer)

- a. Marketspace
- b. Notice and take down
- c. Demandware
- d. Mobile commerce

Guidance: level 1

:: Middleware ::

_____ is computer software that provides services to software applications beyond those available from the operating system. It can be described as "software glue".

Exam Probability: **High**

8. *Answer choices:*

(see index for correct answer)

- a. Middleware
- b. GameSpy Technology
- c. Run-Time Infrastructure
- d. Kynapse

:: World Wide Web ::

_____ LLC is an American multinational technology company that specializes in Internet-related services and products, which include online advertising technologies, search engine, cloud computing, software, and hardware. It is considered one of the Big Four technology companies, alongside Amazon, Apple and Facebook.

Exam Probability: **Medium**

9. *Answer choices:*

(see index for correct answer)

- a. Content development
- b. World Wide Web
- c. Contact page
- d. Hxxp

:: Software design ::

_____ is the process of defining the architecture, modules, interfaces, and data for a system to satisfy specified requirements. _____ could be seen as the application of systems theory to product development. There is some overlap with the disciplines of systems analysis, systems architecture and systems engineering.

Exam Probability: **High**

10. *Answer choices:*

(see index for correct answer)

- a. Systems design
- b. Continuous design
- c. Responsibility-driven design
- d. Interface bloat

Guidance: level 1

:: Data centers ::

A _____ or data centre is a building, dedicated space within a building, or a group of buildings used to house computer systems and associated components, such as telecommunications and storage systems.

Exam Probability: **Low**

11. *Answer choices:*

(see index for correct answer)

- a. Sun Modular Datacenter
- b. Data center
- c. Data center predictive modeling
- d. Fibernet Corp.

Guidance: level 1

:: Software development philosophies ::

A _____ is a method or technique that has been generally accepted as superior to any alternatives because it produces results that are superior to those achieved by other means or because it has become a standard way of doing things, e.g., a standard way of complying with legal or ethical requirements.

Exam Probability: **Low**

12. *Answer choices:*
(see index for correct answer)

- a. Scrum pattern
- b. Best practice
- c. Lean software development
- d. You aren%27t gonna need it

Guidance: level 1

:: Enterprise modelling ::

A _____ or business method is a collection of related, structured activities or tasks by people or equipment which in a specific sequence produce a service or product for a particular customer or customers. _____ es occur at all organizational levels and may or may not be visible to the customers. A _____ may often be visualized as a flowchart of a sequence of activities with interleaving decision points or as a process matrix of a sequence of activities with relevance rules based on data in the process. The benefits of using _____ es include improved customer satisfaction and improved agility for reacting to rapid market change. Process-oriented organizations break down the barriers of structural departments and try to avoid functional silos.

Exam Probability: **Low**

13. *Answer choices:*

(see index for correct answer)

- a. Generalised Enterprise Reference Architecture and Methodology
- b. Business process
- c. Avolution
- d. Real-time Control System

Guidance: level 1

:: Operations research ::

_____ refers to a business or organization attempting to acquire goods or services to accomplish its goals. Although there are several organizations that attempt to set standards in the _____ process, processes can vary greatly between organizations. Typically the word " _____ " is not used interchangeably with the word "procurement", since procurement typically includes expediting, supplier quality, and transportation and logistics in addition to _____ .

Exam Probability: **High**

14. *Answer choices:*

(see index for correct answer)

- a. Operations and technology management
- b. Industrial engineering
- c. Purchasing
- d. The Netherlands Society for Statistics and Operations Research

Guidance: level 1

:: Online analytical processing ::

_____ , or OLAP , is an approach to answer multi-dimensional analytical queries swiftly in computing. OLAP is part of the broader category of business intelligence, which also encompasses relational databases, report writing and data mining. Typical applications of OLAP include business reporting for sales, marketing, management reporting, business process management , budgeting and forecasting, financial reporting and similar areas, with new applications emerging, such as agriculture. The term OLAP was created as a slight modification of the traditional database term online transaction processing .

Exam Probability: **Low**

15. *Answer choices:*

(see index for correct answer)

- a. XML for Analysis
- b. Online analytical processing
- c. IcCube
- d. MOLAP

Guidance: level 1

:: Computer security ::

In the fields of physical security and information security, _____ is the selective restriction of access to a place or other resource. The act of accessing may mean consuming, entering, or using. Permission to access a resource is called authorization.

16. *Answer choices:*

(see index for correct answer)

- a. RFPolicy
- b. Chain of trust
- c. Cyberwarfare
- d. Access control

Guidance: level 1

:: Evaluation methods ::

_____ is asystematic determination of a subject's merit, worth and significance, using criteria governed by a set of standards. It can assist an organization, program, design, project or any other intervention or initiative to assess any aim, realisable concept/proposal, or any alternative, to help in decision-making; or to ascertain the degree of achievement or value in regard to the aim and objectives and results of any such action that has been completed. The primary purpose of _____ , in addition to gaining insight into prior or existing initiatives, is to enable reflection and assist in the identification of future change.

Exam Probability: **Medium**

17. *Answer choices:*

(see index for correct answer)

- a. Educational accreditation
- b. Destructive testing
- c. Evaluation
- d. Educational evaluation

Guidance: level 1

:: Formal languages ::

A _____ is a mark, sign or word that indicates, signifies, or is understood as representing an idea, object, or relationship. _____ s allow people to go beyond what is known or seen by creating linkages between otherwise very different concepts and experiences. All communication is achieved through the use of _____ s. _____ s take the form of words, sounds, gestures, ideas or visual images and are used to convey other ideas and beliefs. For example, a red octagon may be a _____ for "STOP". On a map, a blue line might represent a river. Numerals are _____ s for numbers. Alphabetic letters may be _____ s for sounds. Personal names are _____ s representing individuals. A red rose may _____ ize love and compassion. The variable `x`, in a mathematical equation, may _____ ize the position of a particle in space.

Exam Probability: **High**

18. *Answer choices:*

(see index for correct answer)

- a. Chomsky hierarchy
- b. Symbol

- c. Intended interpretation
- d. Attribute grammar

Guidance: level 1

:: Virtual reality ::

_____ is an experience taking place within simulated and immersive environments that can be similar to or completely different from the real world. Applications of _____ can include entertainment and educational purposes . Other, distinct types of VR style technology include augmented reality and mixed reality.

Exam Probability: **Low**

19. *Answer choices:*

(see index for correct answer)

- a. DirectX
- b. Environmental Audio Extensions
- c. Immersive technology
- d. Virtual reality

Guidance: level 1

:: Cloud clients ::

_____ is a line of smartphones designed and marketed by Apple Inc. All generations of the _____ use Apple's iOS mobile operating system software. The first-generation _____ was released on June 29, 2007, and multiple new hardware iterations with new iOS releases have been released since.

Exam Probability: **Medium**

20. *Answer choices:*

(see index for correct answer)

- a. Zonbu
- b. Replicant
- c. Google Chrome
- d. CloudBook

Guidance: level 1

:: World Wide Web Consortium standards ::

Hypertext Markup Language is the standard markup language for creating web pages and web applications. With Cascading Style Sheets and JavaScript, it forms a triad of cornerstone technologies for the World Wide Web.

Exam Probability: **Medium**

21. *Answer choices:*

(see index for correct answer)

- a. DOM events
- b. Speech Recognition Grammar Specification
- c. Cascading Style Sheets
- d. Html

Guidance: level 1

:: Computer file systems ::

In computing, a _____ or filesystem controls how data is stored and retrieved. Without a _____ , information placed in a storage medium would be one large body of data with no way to tell where one piece of information stops and the next begins. By separating the data into pieces and giving each piece a name, the information is easily isolated and identified. Taking its name from the way paper-based information systems are named, each group of data is called a "file". The structure and logic rules used to manage the groups of information and their names is called a " _____ ".

Exam Probability: **Medium**

22. *Answer choices:*

(see index for correct answer)

- a. File system
- b. Block
- c. Key Sequenced Data Set

- d. Union mount

Guidance: level 1

:: Internet fraud ::

_____ is the act of using a computer to take or alter electronic data, or to gain unlawful use of a computer or system. In the United States, _____ is specifically proscribed by the _____ and Abuse Act, which criminalizes computer-related acts under federal jurisdiction. Types of _____ include.

Exam Probability: **High**

23. *Answer choices:*

(see index for correct answer)

- a. Stock Generation
- b. Artists Against 419
- c. Internet fraud
- d. AllClear ID

Guidance: level 1

:: Artificial intelligence ::

In computer science, _____ , sometimes called machine intelligence, is intelligence demonstrated by machines, in contrast to the natural intelligence displayed by humans and animals. Colloquially, the term " _____ " is used to describe machines that mimic "cognitive" functions that humans associate with other human minds, such as "learning" and "problem solving".

Exam Probability: **High**

24. *Answer choices:*

(see index for correct answer)

- a. GOFAI
- b. Soft computing
- c. Model-based reasoning
- d. Document mosaicing

Guidance: level 1

:: Data management ::

A _____ , or metadata repository, as defined in the IBM Dictionary of Computing, is a "centralized repository of information about data such as meaning, relationships to other data, origin, usage, and format". Oracle defines it as a collection of tables with metadata. The term can have one of several closely related meanings pertaining to databases and database management systems .

Exam Probability: **Medium**

25. *Answer choices:*

- a. Consumer relationship system
- b. Data dictionary
- c. Schema crosswalk
- d. ISO 8000

Guidance: level 1

:: E-commerce ::

Customer to customer markets provide an innovative way to allow customers to interact with each other. Traditional markets require business to customer relationships, in which a customer goes to the business in order to purchase a product or service. In customer to customer markets, the business facilitates an environment where customers can sell goods or services to each other. Other types of markets include business to business and business to customer .

Exam Probability: **Low**

26. *Answer choices:*

- a. Consumer-to-business
- b. Adult Check
- c. Value-added network
- d. Cyber Black Friday

:: Holism ::

_____ characterises the behaviour of a system or model whose components interact in multiple ways and follow local rules, meaning there is no reasonable higher instruction to define the various possible interactions.

Exam Probability: **Medium**

27. *Answer choices:*

(see index for correct answer)

- a. Modular programming
- b. Complexity
- c. Integral theory
- d. Powers of Ten

:: Computer network security ::

An _____ is a controlled private network that allows access to partners, vendors and suppliers or an authorized set of customers – normally to a subset of the information accessible from an organization's intranet. An _____ is similar to a DMZ in that it provides access to needed services for authorized parties, without granting access to an organization's entire network. An _____ is a private network organization.

Exam Probability: **Low**

28. *Answer choices:*

(see index for correct answer)

- a. Wireless security
- b. Cutwail botnet
- c. Extranet
- d. Port knocking

Guidance: level 1

:: Graphical user interface elements ::

A _____ is an opening in a wall, door, roof or vehicle that allows the passage of light, sound, and air. Modern _____ s are usually glazed or covered in some other transparent or translucent material, a sash set in a frame in the opening; the sash and frame are also referred to as a _____ . Many glazed _____ s may be opened, to allow ventilation, or closed, to exclude inclement weather. _____ s often have a latch or similar mechanism to lock the _____ shut or to hold it open by various amounts.

29. *Answer choices:*

(see index for correct answer)

- a. Loading screen
- b. Share icon
- c. Integration tree
- d. Window

Guidance: level 1

:: Data types ::

In linguistics, a _____ is the smallest element that can be uttered in isolation with objective or practical meaning.

Exam Probability: **High**

30. *Answer choices:*

(see index for correct answer)

- a. Word
- b. Weak symbol
- c. Physical address
- d. Variable

:: Software ::

Computer _____ , or simply _____ , is a collection of data or computer instructions that tell the computer how to work. This is in contrast to physical hardware, from which the system is built and actually performs the work. In computer science and _____ engineering, computer _____ is all information processed by computer systems, programs and data. Computer _____ includes computer programs, libraries and related non-executable data, such as online documentation or digital media. Computer hardware and _____ require each other and neither can be realistically used on its own.

Exam Probability: **Medium**

31. *Answer choices:*

(see index for correct answer)

- a. NetSupport School
- b. MacType
- c. Software
- d. Gamma Control

:: Data search engines ::

A web _____ or Internet _____ is a software system that is designed to carry out web search , which means to search the World Wide Web in a systematic way for particular information specified in a web search query. The search results are generally presented in a line of results, often referred to as _____ results pages . The information may be a mix of web pages, images, videos, infographics, articles, research papers and other types of files. Some _____ s also mine data available in databases or open directories. Unlike web directories, which are maintained only by human editors, _____ s also maintain real-time information by running an algorithm on a web crawler.Internet content that is not capable of being searched by a web _____ is generally described as the deep web.

Exam Probability: **High**

32. *Answer choices:*

(see index for correct answer)

- a. Search engine
- b. Multimodal search
- c. Egomath
- d. Voice search

Guidance: level 1

:: Image processing ::

_____ , or colour , is the characteristic of human visual perception described through _____ categories, with names such as red, orange, yellow, green, blue, or purple. This perception of _____ derives from the stimulation of cone cells in the human eye by electromagnetic radiation in the visible spectrum. _____ categories and physical specifications of _____ are associated with objects through the wavelength of the light that is reflected from them. This reflection is governed by the object's physical properties such as light absorption, emission spectra, etc.

Exam Probability: **High**

33. *Answer choices:*

(see index for correct answer)

- a. Color
- b. Shape factor
- c. Pandemonium architecture
- d. Exposure Fusion

Guidance: level 1

:: Groupware ::

Collaborative software or _____ is application software designed to help people involved in a common task to achieve their goals. One of the earliest definitions of collaborative software is "intentional group processes plus software to support them".

34. *Answer choices:*

(see index for correct answer)

- a. MSN Groups
- b. IBM Lotus QuickPlace
- c. Sukey
- d. Ekiga

Guidance: level 1

:: Enterprise application integration ::

_____ is a financial estimate intended to help buyers and owners determine the direct and indirect costs of a product or system. It is a management accounting concept that can be used in full cost accounting or even ecological economics where it includes social costs.

Exam Probability: **High**

35. *Answer choices:*

(see index for correct answer)

- a. Oracle Service Bus
- b. OpenBRR
- c. Convertigo

- d. Total cost of ownership

Guidance: level 1

:: Database management systems ::

A _____ or pillar in architecture and structural engineering is a structural element that transmits, through compression, the weight of the structure above to other structural elements below. In other words, a _____ is a compression member. The term _____ applies especially to a large round support with a capital and a base or pedestal which is made of stone, or appearing to be so. A small wooden or metal support is typically called a post, and supports with a rectangular or other non-round section are usually called piers. For the purpose of wind or earthquake engineering, _____ s may be designed to resist lateral forces. Other compression members are often termed " _____ s" because of the similar stress conditions. _____ s are frequently used to support beams or arches on which the upper parts of walls or ceilings rest. In architecture, " _____ " refers to such a structural element that also has certain proportional and decorative features. A _____ might also be a decorative element not needed for structural purposes; many _____ s are "engaged", that is to say form part of a wall.

Exam Probability: **Medium**

36. *Answer choices:*

(see index for correct answer)

- a. No-force
- b. Superkey
- c. ANSI-SPARC Architecture

- d. Column

Guidance: level 1

:: System software ::

_____ is software designed to provide a platform for other software. Examples of _____ include operating systems like macOS, Ubuntu and Microsoft Windows, computational science software, game engines, industrial automation, and software as a service applications.

Exam Probability: **High**

37. *Answer choices:*

(see index for correct answer)

- a. TechExcel ServiceWise
- b. Verdiem
- c. System software
- d. PowerMAN

Guidance: level 1

:: Reasoning ::

In logic and philosophy, an _____ is a series of statements , called the premises or premisses , intended to determine the degree of truth of another statement, the conclusion. The logical form of an _____ in a natural language can be represented in a symbolic formal language, and independently of natural language formally defined " _____ s" can be made in math and computer science.

Exam Probability: **Low**

38. *Answer choices:*

(see index for correct answer)

- a. Argument
- b. Proportional reasoning
- c. Misology
- d. Knowledge representation

Guidance: level 1

:: Computer memory ::

_____ is the complex cognitive process of decoding symbols to derive meaning. It is a form of language processing.

Exam Probability: **High**

39. *Answer choices:*

(see index for correct answer)

- a. Far pointer
- b. Reading
- c. Regenerative capacitor memory
- d. Flashing

Guidance: level 1

:: Computer security ::

_____ , sometimes shortened to InfoSec, is the practice of preventing unauthorized access, use, disclosure, disruption, modification, inspection, recording or destruction of information. The information or data may take any form, e.g. electronic or physical. _____ 's primary focus is the balanced protection of the confidentiality, integrity and availability of data while maintaining a focus on efficient policy implementation, all without hampering organization productivity. This is largely achieved through a multi-step risk management process that identifies assets, threat sources, vulnerabilities, potential impacts, and possible controls, followed by assessment of the effectiveness of the risk management plan.

Exam Probability: **Low**

40. *Answer choices:*

(see index for correct answer)

- a. Information security
- b. Federal Information Security Management Act of 2002

- c. Gay Nigger Association of America
- d. Centurion guard

Guidance: level 1

:: Computing output devices ::

An _____ is any piece of computer hardware equipment which converts information into human-readable form.

Exam Probability: **Medium**

41. *Answer choices:*

(see index for correct answer)

- a. Output device
- b. MyVu
- c. DR37-P
- d. Powerwall

Guidance: level 1

:: Logic ::

_____ s are mental representations, abstract objects or abilities that make up the fundamental building blocks of thoughts and beliefs. They play an important role in all aspects of cognition.

Exam Probability: **Medium**

42. *Answer choices:*

(see index for correct answer)

- a. Enumerative definition
- b. Concept
- c. Austrian Ludwig Wittgenstein Society
- d. Porphyrian tree

Guidance: level 1

:: Management ::

_____ is the practice of initiating, planning, executing, controlling, and closing the work of a team to achieve specific goals and meet specific success criteria at the specified time.

Exam Probability: **High**

43. *Answer choices:*

(see index for correct answer)

- a. delegation
- b. performance measurement
- c. supply network
- d. Asset management

Guidance: level 1

:: Malware ::

_____ is any software intentionally designed to cause damage to a computer, server, client, or computer network. _____ does the damage after it is implanted or introduced in some way into a target's computer and can take the form of executable code, scripts, active content, and other software. The code is described as computer viruses, worms, Trojan horses, ransomware, spyware, adware, and scareware, among other terms. _____ has a malicious intent, acting against the interest of the computer user—and so does not include software that causes unintentional harm due to some deficiency, which is typically described as a software bug.

Exam Probability: **High**

44. *Answer choices:*

(see index for correct answer)

- a. Malware
- b. Hover ad
- c. Winwebsec
- d. Extended Copy Protection

:: Cryptography ::

In communications and information processing, _____ is a system of rules to convert information—such as a letter, word, sound, image, or gesture—into another form or representation, sometimes shortened or secret, for communication through a communication channel or storage in a storage medium. An early example is the invention of language, which enabled a person, through speech, to communicate what they saw, heard, felt, or thought to others. But speech limits the range of communication to the distance a voice can carry, and limits the audience to those present when the speech is uttered. The invention of writing, which converted spoken language into visual symbols, extended the range of communication across space and time.

Exam Probability: **Medium**

45. *Answer choices:*

(see index for correct answer)

- a. Enigma machine
- b. Security association
- c. Convergent encryption
- d. Code

:: E-commerce ::

B2B is often contrasted with business-to-consumer . In B2B commerce, it is often the case that the parties to the relationship have comparable negotiating power, and even when they do not, each party typically involves professional staff and legal counsel in the negotiation of terms, whereas B2C is shaped to a far greater degree by economic implications of information asymmetry. However, within a B2B context, large companies may have many commercial, resource and information advantages over smaller businesses. The United Kingdom government, for example, created the post of Small Business Commissioner under the Enterprise Act 2016 to "enable small businesses to resolve disputes" and "consider complaints by small business suppliers about payment issues with larger businesses that they supply."

Exam Probability: **High**

46. *Answer choices:*

(see index for correct answer)

- a. Open Market
- b. Business-to-business
- c. Internet booking engine
- d. Conversion as a service

Guidance: level 1

:: Computer memory ::

_____ is a type of non-volatile memory used in computers and other electronic devices. Data stored in ROM can only be modified slowly, with difficulty, or not at all, so it is mainly used to store firmware or application software in plug-in cartridges.

Exam Probability: **High**

47. *Answer choices:*

(see index for correct answer)

- a. Shadow RAM
- b. Read-only memory
- c. Working set size
- d. Page cache

Guidance: level 1

:: E-commerce ::

_____ is the activity of buying or selling of products on online services or over the Internet. Electronic commerce draws on technologies such as mobile commerce, electronic funds transfer, supply chain management, Internet marketing, online transaction processing, electronic data interchange , inventory management systems, and automated data collection systems.

Exam Probability: **Low**

48. *Answer choices:*

(see index for correct answer)

- a. E-commerce
- b. Yemeksepeti
- c. Mobile banking
- d. Freelance marketplace

Guidance: level 1

:: Operating systems ::

An _____ is system software that manages computer hardware and software resources and provides common services for computer programs.

Exam Probability: **Medium**

49. *Answer choices:*

(see index for correct answer)

- a. Supercomputer operating systems
- b. Operating System Patcher
- c. VM/386
- d. Operating system

Guidance: level 1

:: Knowledge engineering ::

A _____ is an information system that supports business or organizational decision-making activities. DSSs serve the management, operations and planning levels of an organization and help people make decisions about problems that may be rapidly changing and not easily specified in advance—i.e. unstructured and semi-structured decision problems. _____ s can be either fully computerized or human-powered, or a combination of both.

Exam Probability: **High**

50. *Answer choices:*

(see index for correct answer)

- a. Subject-matter expert
- b. DriveWorks
- c. NetWeaver Developer
- d. Frame language

Guidance: level 1

:: Integrated development environments ::

_____ is a third-generation event-driven programming language from Microsoft for its Component Object Model programming model first released in 1991 and declared legacy during 2008. Microsoft intended _____ to be relatively easy to learn and use. _____ was derived from BASIC and enables the rapid application development of graphical user interface applications, access to databases using Data Access Objects, Remote Data Objects, or ActiveX Data Objects, and creation of ActiveX controls and objects.

Exam Probability: **Medium**

51. *Answer choices:*

(see index for correct answer)

- a. PyCharm
- b. Visual Basic
- c. MyEclipse
- d. Basic4ppc

Guidance: level 1

:: Spreadsheet software ::

A _____ is an interactive computer application for organization, analysis and storage of data in tabular form. _____ s developed as computerized analogs of paper accounting worksheets. The program operates on data entered in cells of a table. Each cell may contain either numeric or text data, or the results of formulas that automatically calculate and display a value based on the contents of other cells. A _____ may also refer to one such electronic document.

52. *Answer choices:*

(see index for correct answer)

- a. Logical spreadsheet
- b. Spreadsheet
- c. As Easy As
- d. Pivot table

Guidance: level 1

:: Artificial intelligence ::

In artificial intelligence, an _____ is a computer system that emulates the decision-making ability of a human expert. _____ s are designed to solve complex problems by reasoning through bodies of knowledge, represented mainly as if–then rules rather than through conventional procedural code. The first _____ s were created in the 1970s and then proliferated in the 1980s. _____ s were among the first truly successful forms of artificial intelligence software. However, some experts point out that _____ s were not part of true artificial intelligence since they lack the ability to learn autonomously from external data. An _____ is divided into two subsystems: the inference engine and the knowledge base. The knowledge base represents facts and rules. The inference engine applies the rules to the known facts to deduce new facts. Inference engines can also include explanation and debugging abilities.

Answer choices:

(see index for correct answer)

- a. Soft computing
- b. Embodied cognitive science
- c. Computational creativity
- d. Expert system

Guidance: level 1

:: Mathematical logic ::

_____ is an arrangement and organization of interrelated elements in a material object or system, or the object or system so organized. Material _____ s include man-made objects such as buildings and machines and natural objects such as biological organisms, minerals and chemicals. Abstract _____ s include data _____ s in computer science and musical form. Types of _____ include a hierarchy , a network featuring many-to-many links, or a lattice featuring connections between components that are neighbors in space.

Exam Probability: **Medium**

54. *Answer choices:*

(see index for correct answer)

- a. Structure
- b. Contraposition

- c. Model theory
- d. Finitary

Guidance: level 1

:: Cloud applications ::

_____ is a software licensing and delivery model in which software is licensed on a subscription basis and is centrally hosted. It is sometimes referred to as "on-demand software", and was formerly referred to as "software plus services" by Microsoft. SaaS is typically accessed by users using a thin client, e.g. via a web browser. SaaS has become a common delivery model for many business applications, including office software, messaging software, payroll processing software, DBMS software, management software, CAD software, development software, gamification, virtualization, accounting, collaboration, customer relationship management , Management Information Systems , enterprise resource planning , invoicing, human resource management , talent acquisition, learning management systems, content management , Geographic Information Systems , and service desk management. SaaS has been incorporated into the strategy of nearly all leading enterprise software companies.

Exam Probability: **High**

55. *Answer choices:*
(see index for correct answer)

- a. IKnowWare
- b. SmartFocus
- c. Artist Growth
- d. Software as a service

:: Workflow technology ::

A _____ consists of an orchestrated and repeatable pattern of business activity enabled by the systematic organization of resources into processes that transform materials, provide services, or process information. It can be depicted as a sequence of operations, the work of a person or group, the work of an organization of staff, or one or more simple or complex mechanisms.

Exam Probability: **Medium**

56. *Answer choices:*

(see index for correct answer)

- a. Workflow technology
- b. Neural Workflow
- c. Workflow
- d. Discovery Net

:: Data security ::

In financial accounting, an _____ is any resource owned by the business. Anything tangible or intangible that can be owned or controlled to produce value and that is held by a company to produce positive economic value is an _____ . Simply stated, _____ s represent value of ownership that can be converted into cash . The balance sheet of a firm records the monetary value of the _____ s owned by that firm. It covers money and other valuables belonging to an individual or to a business.

Exam Probability: **Medium**

57. *Answer choices:*

(see index for correct answer)

- a. Transshipment
- b. Splunk
- c. Asset
- d. Defense in depth

Guidance: level 1

:: Malware ::

The _____ is a story from the Trojan War about the subterfuge that the Greeks used to enter the independent city of Troy and win the war. In the canonical version, after a fruitless 10-year siege, the Greeks constructed a huge wooden horse, and hid a select force of men inside including Odysseus. The Greeks pretended to sail away, and the Trojans pulled the horse into their city as a victory trophy. That night the Greek force crept out of the horse and opened the gates for the rest of the Greek army, which had sailed back under cover of night. The Greeks entered and destroyed the city of Troy, ending the war.

Exam Probability: **High**

58. *Answer choices:*

(see index for correct answer)

- a. Cyberweapon
- b. Trojan horse
- c. Patched
- d. Fraudtool

Guidance: level 1

:: History of the Internet ::

Electronic mail is a method of exchanging messages between people using electronic devices. Invented by Ray Tomlinson, _____ first entered limited use in the 1960s and by the mid-1970s had taken the form now recognized as _____ . _____ operates across computer networks, which today is primarily the Internet. Some early _____ systems required the author and the recipient to both be online at the same time, in common with instant messaging. Today's _____ systems are based on a store-and-forward model. _____ servers accept, forward, deliver, and store messages. Neither the users nor their computers are required to be online simultaneously; they need to connect only briefly, typically to a mail server or a webmail interface for as long as it takes to send or receive messages.

Exam Probability: **Medium**

59. *Answer choices:*

(see index for correct answer)

- a. InterNIC
- b. MIDnet
- c. Next Generation Internet Program
- d. Minitel

Guidance: level 1

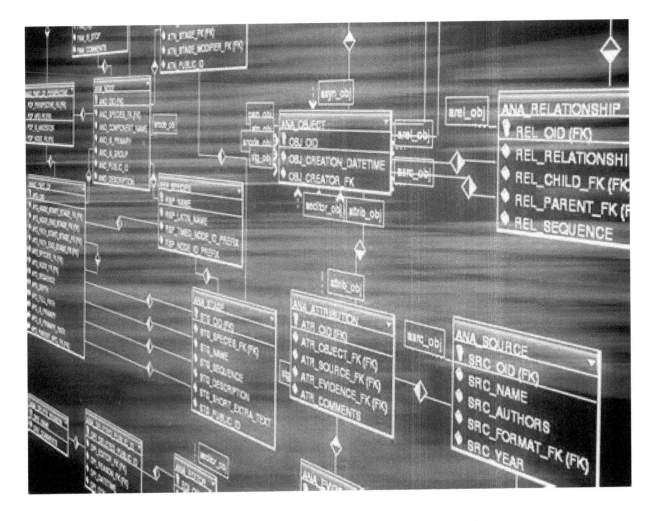

Database management

A database is an organized collection of data, generally stored and accessed electronically from a computer system. The database management system is the software that interacts with end users, applications, and the database itself to capture and analyze the data. The DBMS software additionally encompasses the core facilities provided to administer the database. The sum total of the database, the DBMS and the associated applications can be referred to as a "database system".

:: Database index techniques ::

In computer science, a _____ is a self-balancing tree data structure that maintains sorted data and allows searches, sequential access, insertions, and deletions in logarithmic time. The _____ is a generalization of a binary search tree in that a node can have more than two children. Unlike other self-balancing binary search trees, the _____ is well suited for storage systems that read and write relatively large blocks of data, such as discs. It is commonly used in databases and file systems.

Exam Probability: **Low**

1. *Answer choices:*

(see index for correct answer)

- a. X-tree
- b. Compressed suffix array
- c. Log-structured merge-tree
- d. B-tree

Guidance: level 1

:: Database models ::

The _____ is a database model conceived as a flexible way of representing objects and their relationships. Its distinguishing feature is that the schema, viewed as a graph in which object types are nodes and relationship types are arcs, is not restricted to being a hierarchy or lattice.

Exam Probability: **Medium**

2. *Answer choices:*

(see index for correct answer)

- a. Hierarchical database model
- b. Flat file database
- c. Component-oriented database
- d. Semi-structured model

Guidance: level 1

:: Data management ::

A _____ , or metadata repository, as defined in the IBM Dictionary of Computing, is a "centralized repository of information about data such as meaning, relationships to other data, origin, usage, and format". Oracle defines it as a collection of tables with metadata. The term can have one of several closely related meanings pertaining to databases and database management systems .

Exam Probability: **Low**

3. *Answer choices:*

(see index for correct answer)

- a. Data dictionary
- b. Master data
- c. Very large database
- d. Navigational database

:: Database normalization ::

_____ is a normal form used in database normalization. 2NF was originally defined by E.F. Codd in 1971.

Exam Probability: **High**

4. *Answer choices:*

(see index for correct answer)

- a. Single version of the truth
- b. Third normal form
- c. Second normal form
- d. Join dependency

:: Data warehousing ::

In data warehousing, a _____ consists of the measurements, metrics or facts of a business process. It is located at the center of a star schema or a snowflake schema surrounded by dimension tables. Where multiple _____ s are used, these are arranged as a fact constellation schema. A _____ typically has two types of columns: those that contain facts and those that are a foreign key to dimension tables. The primary key of a _____ is usually a composite key that is made up of all of its foreign keys. _____ s contain the content of the data warehouse and store different types of measures like additive, non additive, and semi additive measures.

Exam Probability: **Medium**

5. *Answer choices:*

(see index for correct answer)

- a. Fact table
- b. Ralph Kimball
- c. Aggregate
- d. Data warehouse appliance

Guidance: level 1

:: Data security ::

In financial accounting, an _____ is any resource owned by the business. Anything tangible or intangible that can be owned or controlled to produce value and that is held by a company to produce positive economic value is an _____ . Simply stated, _____ s represent value of ownership that can be converted into cash . The balance sheet of a firm records the monetary value of the _____ s owned by that firm. It covers money and other valuables belonging to an individual or to a business.

Exam Probability: **High**

6. *Answer choices:*

(see index for correct answer)

- a. Loss of United Kingdom child benefit data
- b. Signed and Encrypted Email Over The Internet
- c. Asset
- d. Blancco

Guidance: level 1

:: Computer programming ::

In computing, Open Database Connectivity is a standard application programming interface for accessing database management systems . The designers of _____ aimed to make it independent of database systems and operating systems. An application written using _____ can be ported to other platforms, both on the client and server side, with few changes to the data access code.

Exam Probability: **Low**

7. *Answer choices:*

(see index for correct answer)

- a. Grist
- b. End-user development
- c. Polyglot
- d. Gerrit

Guidance: level 1

:: Database normalization ::

_____ , also known as project-join normal form , is a level of database normalization designed to reduce redundancy in relational databases recording multi-valued facts by isolating semantically related multiple relationships. A table is said to be in the 5NF if and only if every non-trivial join dependency in that table is implied by the candidate keys.

Exam Probability: **High**

8. *Answer choices:*

(see index for correct answer)

- a. Bitemporal Modeling
- b. Third normal form

- c. Single Source of Truth
- d. Fifth normal form

Guidance: level 1

:: Databases ::

In the context of relational databases, a _____ is a field in one table that uniquely identifies a row of another table or the same table. In simpler words, the _____ is defined in a second table, but it refers to the primary key or a unique key in the first table. For example, a table called Employees has a primary key called employee_id. Another table called Employee Details has a _____ which references employee_id in order to uniquely identify the relationship between the two tables.

Exam Probability: **Medium**

9. *Answer choices:*

(see index for correct answer)

- a. Elasticity
- b. DataEase
- c. ADO.NET
- d. Foreign key

Guidance: level 1

:: Databases ::

A _____ is a server which houses a database application that provides database services to other computer programs or to computers, as defined by the client–server model. Database management systems frequently provide database-server functionality, and some database management systems rely exclusively on the client–server model for database access .

Exam Probability: **Medium**

10. *Answer choices:*

(see index for correct answer)

- a. Metadatabase
- b. Two-phase locking
- c. Database server
- d. Enterprise database management

Guidance: level 1

:: Database management systems ::

_____ is a class of relational database management systems that seek to provide the scalability of NoSQL systems for online transaction processing workloads while maintaining the ACID guarantees of a traditional database system.

11. *Answer choices:*

(see index for correct answer)

- a. Content repository API for Java
- b. NewSQL
- c. Transaction time
- d. Row

Guidance: level 1

:: Data types ::

In linguistics, a _____ is the smallest element that can be uttered in isolation with objective or practical meaning.

12. *Answer choices:*

(see index for correct answer)

- a. Data type
- b. Word
- c. Latent typing
- d. Physical address

:: Database management systems ::

_____ is a proprietary multi-model database management system produced and marketed by Oracle Corporation.

Exam Probability: **Medium**

13. *Answer choices:*

(see index for correct answer)

- a. ISBL
- b. Oracle Database
- c. Database transaction
- d. Distributed database

:: Bit data structures ::

In computing, a _____ is a mapping from some domain to bits. It is also called a bit array or _____ index.

14. *Answer choices:*

(see index for correct answer)

- a. Bit field
- b. Bit plane
- c. Bitmap

Guidance: level 1

:: Operations research ::

_____ refers to a business or organization attempting to acquire goods or services to accomplish its goals. Although there are several organizations that attempt to set standards in the _____ process, processes can vary greatly between organizations. Typically the word " _____ " is not used interchangeably with the word "procurement", since procurement typically includes expediting, supplier quality, and transportation and logistics in addition to _____ .

Exam Probability: **High**

15. *Answer choices:*

(see index for correct answer)

- a. Berth allocation problem
- b. Proaftn

- c. Marketing science
- d. Generalized assignment problem

Guidance: level 1

:: Online analytical processing ::

_____ , or OLAP , is an approach to answer multi-dimensional analytical queries swiftly in computing. OLAP is part of the broader category of business intelligence, which also encompasses relational databases, report writing and data mining. Typical applications of OLAP include business reporting for sales, marketing, management reporting, business process management , budgeting and forecasting, financial reporting and similar areas, with new applications emerging, such as agriculture. The term OLAP was created as a slight modification of the traditional database term online transaction processing .

Exam Probability: **High**

16. *Answer choices:*

(see index for correct answer)

- a. FASMI
- b. Online analytical processing
- c. Snowflake schema
- d. XLCubed

Guidance: level 1

:: Data security ::

In computer science, _____ is the process of ensuring data have undergone data cleansing to ensure they have data quality, that is, that they are both correct and useful. It uses routines, often called "validation rules" "validation constraints" or "check routines", that check for correctness, meaningfulness, and security of data that are input to the system. The rules may be implemented through the automated facilities of a data dictionary, or by the inclusion of explicit application program validation logic.

Exam Probability: **Low**

17. *Answer choices:*

(see index for correct answer)

- a. Data validation
- b. Information repository
- c. Single loss expectancy
- d. Crypto cloud computing

Guidance: level 1

:: Databases ::

In databases and transaction processing, _____ is a concurrency control method that guarantees serializability. It is also the name of the resulting set of database transaction schedules. The protocol utilizes locks, applied by a transaction to data, which may block other transactions from accessing the same data during the transaction's life.

Exam Probability: **High**

18. *Answer choices:*

(see index for correct answer)

- a. IDMS
- b. Relvar
- c. Two-phase locking
- d. Commitment ordering

Guidance: level 1

:: Data quality ::

_____ refers to the condition of a set of values of qualitative or quantitative variables. There are many definitions of _____ but data is generally considered high quality if it is "fit for [its] intended uses in operations, decision making and planning". Alternatively, data is deemed of high quality if it correctly represents the real-world construct to which it refers. Furthermore, apart from these definitions, as data volume increases, the question of internal data consistency becomes significant, regardless of fitness for use for any particular external purpose. People's views on _____ can often be in disagreement, even when discussing the same set of data used for the same purpose. Data cleansing may be required in order to ensure _____ .

Exam Probability: **High**

19. *Answer choices:*

(see index for correct answer)

- a. One-for-one checking
- b. Data quality assurance
- c. Data Quality Firewall
- d. Data quality

Guidance: level 1

:: Database management systems ::

_____ is a function of many relational database management systems. The query optimizer attempts to determine the most efficient way to execute a given query by considering the possible query plans.

20. *Answer choices:*

(see index for correct answer)

- a. Surrogate key
- b. Valid time
- c. Column
- d. Column-oriented DBMS

Guidance: level 1

:: Fault-tolerant computer systems ::

Transaction processing is information processing in computer science that is divided into individual, indivisible operations called transactions. Each transaction must succeed or fail as a complete unit; it can never be only partially complete.

Exam Probability: **Low**

21. *Answer choices:*

(see index for correct answer)

- a. Failure detector
- b. Virtual Link Trunking
- c. Replication

- d. Round-robin DNS

Guidance: level 1

:: Online analytical processing ::

An _____ is a multi-dimensional array of data. Online analytical processing is a computer-based technique of analyzing data to look for insights. The term cube here refers to a multi-dimensional dataset, which is also sometimes called a hypercube if the number of dimensions is greater than 3.

Exam Probability: **High**

22. *Answer choices:*
(see index for correct answer)

- a. XML for Analysis
- b. Palo
- c. Panorama Software
- d. OLAP cube

Guidance: level 1

:: Mereology ::

_____ , in the abstract, is what belongs to or with something, whether as an attribute or as a component of said thing. In the context of this article, it is one or more components , whether physical or incorporeal, of a person's estate; or so belonging to, as in being owned by, a person or jointly a group of people or a legal entity like a corporation or even a society. Depending on the nature of the _____ , an owner of _____ has the right to consume, alter, share, redefine, rent, mortgage, pawn, sell, exchange, transfer, give away or destroy it, or to exclude others from doing these things, as well as to perhaps abandon it; whereas regardless of the nature of the _____ , the owner thereof has the right to properly use it , or at the very least exclusively keep it.

Exam Probability: **Medium**

23. *Answer choices:*

(see index for correct answer)

- a. Mereological essentialism
- b. Meronomy
- c. Non-wellfounded mereology
- d. Property

Guidance: level 1

:: Databases ::

In concurrency control of databases, transaction processing , and various transactional applications , both centralized and distributed, a transaction schedule is serializable if its outcome is equal to the outcome of its transactions executed serially, i.e. without overlapping in time. Transactions are normally executed concurrently , since this is the most efficient way.

_____ is the major correctness criterion for concurrent transactions' executions. It is considered the highest level of isolation between transactions, and plays an essential role in concurrency control. As such it is supported in all general purpose database systems. Strong strict two-phase locking is a popular _____ mechanism utilized in most of the database systems since their early days in the 1970s.

Exam Probability: **High**

24. *Answer choices:*

(see index for correct answer)

- a. Data event
- b. Serializability
- c. Database-as-IPC
- d. Database index

Guidance: level 1

:: Database management systems ::

A _____ database provides a mechanism for storage and retrieval of data that is modeled in means other than the tabular relations used in relational databases. Such databases have existed since the late 1960s, but did not obtain the " _____ " moniker until a surge of popularity in the early 21st century, triggered by the needs of Web 2.0 companies. _____ databases are increasingly used in big data and real-time web applications. _____ systems are also sometimes called "Not only SQL" to emphasize that they may support SQL-like query languages, or sit alongside SQL database in a polyglot persistence architecture.

Exam Probability: **Low**

25. *Answer choices:*

(see index for correct answer)

- a. NoSQL
- b. Correlation database
- c. Column-oriented DBMS
- d. Block contention

Guidance: level 1

:: Database management systems ::

A data definition or data description language is a syntax similar to a computer programming language for defining data structures, especially database schemas. DDL statements create, modify, and remove database objects such as tables, indexes, and users. Common DDL statements are CREATE, ALTER, and DROP

26. *Answer choices:*

(see index for correct answer)

- a. Terminfo
- b. Transaction Control Language
- c. Data Definition Language
- d. Oracle Exadata

Guidance: level 1

:: Relational model ::

In a relational database, a _____ is an entity that cannot be uniquely identified by its attributes alone; therefore, it must use a foreign key in conjunction with its attributes to create a primary key. The foreign key is typically a primary key of an entity it is related to.

Exam Probability: **Low**

27. *Answer choices:*

(see index for correct answer)

- a. Weak entity
- b. Recursive join
- c. Polymorphic association

- d. Relational data mining

Guidance: level 1

:: Database normalization ::

_____ is a strategy used on a previously-normalized database to increase performance. In computing, _____ is the process of trying to improve the read performance of a database, at the expense of losing some write performance, by adding redundant copies of data or by grouping data. It is often motivated by performance or scalability in relational database software needing to carry out very large numbers of read operations. _____ should not be confused with Unnormalized form. Databases/tables must first be normalized to efficiently denormalize them.

Exam Probability: **Low**

28. *Answer choices:*

(see index for correct answer)

- a. Domain/key normal form
- b. Sixth normal form
- c. Denormalization
- d. Join dependency

Guidance: level 1

:: Middleware ::

_____ is computer software that provides services to software applications beyond those available from the operating system. It can be described as "software glue".

Exam Probability: **High**

29. *Answer choices:*

(see index for correct answer)

- a. CRI Middleware
- b. Distributed object middleware
- c. Middleware
- d. HyperCast

Guidance: level 1

:: Database security ::

_____ is a key issue in a Real time, we know that all our data is some where store in database. _____ concerns the use of a broad range of information security controls to protect databases against compromises of their confidentiality, integrity and availability. It involves various types or categories of controls, such as technical, procedural/administrative and physical. _____ is a specialist topic within the broader realms of computer security, information security and risk management.

30. *Answer choices:*

(see index for correct answer)

- a. Negative database
- b. Database security
- c. Database forensics

Guidance: level 1

:: Transaction processing ::

Some scenarios associate "this kind of planning" with learning "life skills".
_____ s are necessary, or at least useful, in situations where individuals
need to know what time they must be at a specific location to receive a
specific service, and where people need to accomplish a set of goals within a
set time period.

Exam Probability: **Low**

31. *Answer choices:*

(see index for correct answer)

- a. Purchase-to-pay
- b. Schedule
- c. Data integrity

- d. Transactional NTFS

:: Software ::

Computer _____ , or simply _____ , is a collection of data or computer instructions that tell the computer how to work. This is in contrast to physical hardware, from which the system is built and actually performs the work. In computer science and _____ engineering, computer _____ is all information processed by computer systems, programs and data. Computer _____ includes computer programs, libraries and related non-executable data, such as online documentation or digital media. Computer hardware and _____ require each other and neither can be realistically used on its own.

Exam Probability: **Medium**

32. *Answer choices:*

(see index for correct answer)

- a. Software categories
- b. Software
- c. Video renderer
- d. Topincs

:: Data structures ::

In computer science, a _____ is a tree data structure used for locating specific keys from within a set. In order for a tree to function as a _____ , the key for each node must be greater than any keys in subtrees on the left and less than any keys in subtrees on the right.

Exam Probability: **Low**

33. *Answer choices:*

(see index for correct answer)

- a. Succinct data structure
- b. Search tree
- c. Array data structure
- d. Process Environment Block

Guidance: level 1

:: Strategy ::

_____ is a high level plan to achieve one or more goals under conditions of uncertainty. In the sense of the "art of the general," which included several subsets of skills including tactics, siegecraft, logistics etc., the term came into use in the 6th century C.E. in East Roman terminology, and was translated into Western vernacular languages only in the 18th century. From then until the 20th century, the word "_____" came to denote "a comprehensive way to try to pursue political ends, including the threat or actual use of force, in a dialectic of wills" in a military conflict, in which both adversaries interact.

Exam Probability: **Medium**

34. *Answer choices:*

(see index for correct answer)

- a. SpyParty
- b. Strategic Initiative
- c. Chaotics
- d. Institute for the Analysis of Global Security

Guidance: level 1

:: Formal languages ::

A _____ is a mark, sign or word that indicates, signifies, or is understood as representing an idea, object, or relationship. _____ s allow people to go beyond what is known or seen by creating linkages between otherwise very different concepts and experiences. All communication is achieved through the use of _____ s. _____ s take the form of words, sounds, gestures, ideas or visual images and are used to convey other ideas and beliefs. For example, a red octagon may be a _____ for "STOP". On a map, a blue line might represent a river. Numerals are _____ s for numbers. Alphabetic letters may be _____ s for sounds. Personal names are _____ s representing individuals. A red rose may _____ ize love and compassion. The variable `x`, in a mathematical equation, may _____ ize the position of a particle in space.

Exam Probability: **Low**

35. *Answer choices:*

(see index for correct answer)

- a. Symbol
- b. Abstract family of acceptors
- c. Parser combinator
- d. Markup language

Guidance: level 1

:: Data modeling ::

In the relational model of databases, a _____ is a specific choice of a minimal set of attributes that uniquely specify a tuple in a relation . Informally, a _____ is "which attributes identify a record", and in simple cases are simply a single attribute: a unique id. More formally, a _____ is a choice of candidate key ; any other candidate key is an alternate key.

Exam Probability: **High**

36. *Answer choices:*

(see index for correct answer)

- a. Information model
- b. Object Definition Language
- c. Corticon
- d. IDEF1X

Guidance: level 1

:: Mathematical logic ::

_____ is an arrangement and organization of interrelated elements in a material object or system, or the object or system so organized. Material _____ s include man-made objects such as buildings and machines and natural objects such as biological organisms, minerals and chemicals. Abstract _____ s include data _____ s in computer science and musical form. Types of _____ include a hierarchy , a network featuring many-to-many links, or a lattice featuring connections between components that are neighbors in space.

37. *Answer choices:*

(see index for correct answer)

- a. Predicate
- b. Contraposition
- c. Proof theory
- d. Quantum logic

Guidance: level 1

:: Database management systems ::

A _____ is a computer programming language used for adding , deleting, and modifying data in a database. A DML is often a sublanguage of a broader database language such as SQL, with the DML comprising some of the operators in the language. Read-only selecting of data is sometimes distinguished as being part of a separate data query language , but it is closely related and sometimes also considered a component of a DML; some operators may perform both selecting and writing.

Exam Probability: **High**

38. *Answer choices:*

(see index for correct answer)

- a. Object-based spatial database

- b. Stored procedure
- c. Data Manipulation Language
- d. Relational algebra

Guidance: level 1

:: Scientific method ::

The _____ or method is a proposed description of scientific method. According to it, scientific inquiry proceeds by formulating a hypothesis in a form that can be falsifiable, using a test on observable data where the outcome is not yet known. A test outcome that could have and does run contrary to predictions of the hypothesis is taken as a falsification of the hypothesis. A test outcome that could have, but does not run contrary to the hypothesis corroborates the theory. It is then proposed to compare the explanatory value of competing hypotheses by testing how stringently they are corroborated by their predictions.

Exam Probability: **Medium**

39. *Answer choices:*

(see index for correct answer)

- a. Scientific control
- b. Isotope dilution
- c. Retrodiction
- d. Pilot experiment

Guidance: level 1

:: SQL keywords ::

An <code> _____ </code> clause in SQL specifies that a SQL <code>SELECT</code> statement returns a result set with the rows being sorted by the values of one or more columns. The sort criteria do not have to be included in the result set. The sort criteria can be expressions, including column names, user-defined functions, arithmetic operations, or <code>CASE</code> expressions. The expressions are evaluated and the results are used for the sorting, i.e., the values stored in the column or the results of the function call.

Exam Probability: **Low**

40. *Answer choices:*

(see index for correct answer)

- a. Insert
- b. Order by
- c. Null
- d. Join

Guidance: level 1

:: Database management systems ::

In the field of databases in computer science, a _____ is a history of actions executed by a database management system used to guarantee ACID properties over crashes or hardware failures. Physically, a log is a file listing changes to the database, stored in a stable storage format.

Exam Probability: **High**

41. *Answer choices:*

(see index for correct answer)

- a. Transaction log
- b. Object-based spatial database
- c. Transaction time
- d. Data Description Specifications

Guidance: level 1

:: Databases ::

A _____ is a computer program whose primary purpose is entering and retrieving information from a computerized database. Early examples of _____ s were accounting systems and airline reservations systems, such as SABRE, developed starting in 1957.

Exam Probability: **Low**

42. *Answer choices:*

(see index for correct answer)

- a. Termcap
- b. Modular concurrency control
- c. Aerospike database
- d. Binary large object

Guidance: level 1

:: Database management systems ::

A _____ is a storage location where the actual data underlying database objects can be kept. It provides a layer of abstraction between physical and logical data, and serves to allocate storage for all DBMS managed segments. Once created, a _____ can be referred to by name when creating database segments.

Exam Probability: **Low**

43. *Answer choices:*

(see index for correct answer)

- a. Relational calculus
- b. Object Exchange Model
- c. Superkey
- d. Tablespace

:: Database constraints ::

In relational database theory, a _____ is a constraint between two sets of attributes in a relation from a database. In other words, _____ is between attributes in a relation.

Exam Probability: **High**

44. *Answer choices:*

(see index for correct answer)

- a. Functional dependency
- b. Dependency theory
- c. Transitive dependency

:: Formal languages ::

In computer text processing, a _____ is a system for annotating a document in a way that is syntactically distinguishable from the text. The idea and terminology evolved from the "marking up" of paper manuscripts, i.e., the revision instructions by editors, traditionally written with a red or blue pencil on authors' manuscripts. In digital media this "blue pencil instruction text" was replaced by tags, which indicate what the parts of the document are, rather than details of how they might be shown on some display. This lets authors avoid formatting every instance of the same kind of thing redundantly . It also avoids the specification of fonts and dimensions, which may not apply to many users .

Exam Probability: **High**

45. *Answer choices:*

(see index for correct answer)

- a. Markup language
- b. Growing context-sensitive grammar
- c. Prefix grammar
- d. Regular tree grammar

Guidance: level 1

:: Database management systems ::

A _____ is a type of data model that determines the logical structure of a database and fundamentally determines in which manner data can be stored, organized and manipulated. The most popular example of a _____ is the relational model, which uses a table-based format.

46. *Answer choices:*

(see index for correct answer)

- a. Database model
- b. NoSQL
- c. View
- d. Transaction log

Guidance: level 1

:: Online analytical processing ::

In computing, a _____ is a logical arrangement of tables in a multidimensional database such that the entity relationship diagram resembles a snowflake shape. The _____ is represented by centralized fact tables which are connected to multiple dimensions.. "Snowflaking" is a method of normalizing the dimension tables in a star schema. When it is completely normalized along all the dimension tables, the resultant structure resembles a snowflake with the fact table in the middle. The principle behind snowflaking is normalization of the dimension tables by removing low cardinality attributes and forming separate tables.

Exam Probability: **Low**

47. *Answer choices:*

(see index for correct answer)

- a. FASMI
- b. XLCubed
- c. HOLAP
- d. Palo

Guidance: level 1

:: Database management systems ::

_____ consists of two calculi, the tuple _____ and the domain _____ , that are part of the relational model for databases and provide a declarative way to specify database queries. This in contrast to the relational algebra, which is also part of the relational model but provides a more procedural way for specifying queries.

Exam Probability: **High**

48. *Answer choices:*

(see index for correct answer)

- a. Bitemporal data
- b. ISBL
- c. Big data
- d. Relational calculus

Guidance: level 1

:: Data management ::

In mathematics, a _____ is a finite ordered list of elements. An n-_____ is a sequence of n elements, where n is a non-negative integer. There is only one 0-_____ , an empty sequence, or empty _____ , as it is referred to. An n-_____ is defined inductively using the construction of an ordered pair.

Exam Probability: **Low**

49. *Answer choices:*

(see index for correct answer)

- a. Tuple
- b. Data exchange
- c. Data conditioning
- d. Storage block

Guidance: level 1

:: Reasoning ::

In logic and philosophy, an _____ is a series of statements , called the premises or premisses , intended to determine the degree of truth of another statement, the conclusion. The logical form of an _____ in a natural language can be represented in a symbolic formal language, and independently of natural language formally defined " _____ s" can be made in math and computer science.

50. *Answer choices:*

(see index for correct answer)

- a. Journal of Formalized Reasoning
- b. Practical reason
- c. Argument
- d. Emotional reasoning

Guidance: level 1

:: Big data ::

_____ Corporation is a provider of database and analytics-related software, products, and services. The company was formed in 1979 in Brentwood, California, as a collaboration between researchers at Caltech and Citibank's advanced technology group.

Exam Probability: **High**

51. *Answer choices:*

(see index for correct answer)

- a. Talend
- b. Prescriptive analytics
- c. Hue

- d. Medio

Guidance: level 1

:: Online analytical processing ::

Online analytical processing, or OLAP , is an approach to answer multi-dimensional analytical queries swiftly in computing. OLAP is part of the broader category of business intelligence, which also encompasses relational databases, report writing and data mining. Typical applications of OLAP include business reporting for sales, marketing, management reporting, business process management , budgeting and forecasting, financial reporting and similar areas, with new applications emerging, such as agriculture. The term OLAP was created as a slight modification of the traditional database term online transaction processing .

Exam Probability: **Medium**

52. *Answer choices:*

(see index for correct answer)

- a. ROLAP
- b. MicroStrategy
- c. Applix
- d. Palo

Guidance: level 1

:: Operating systems ::

An _____ is system software that manages computer hardware and software resources and provides common services for computer programs.

Exam Probability: **Medium**

53. *Answer choices:*

(see index for correct answer)

- a. XB Machine
- b. Operating system
- c. Comparison of operating systems
- d. Usage share of operating systems

Guidance: level 1

:: Data structures ::

In computer science, a _____ is a data organization, management, and storage format that enables efficient access and modification. More precisely, a _____ is a collection of data values, the relationships among them, and the functions or operations that can be applied to the data.

Exam Probability: **Medium**

54. *Answer choices:*

(see index for correct answer)

- a. Hash table
- b. Control table
- c. Data structure
- d. Binary tree

Guidance: level 1

:: Database management systems ::

" _____ " is a field that treats ways to analyze, systematically extract information from, or otherwise deal with data sets that are too large or complex to be dealt with by traditional data-processing application software. Data with many cases offer greater statistical power, while data with higher complexity may lead to a higher false discovery rate. _____ challenges include capturing data, data storage, data analysis, search, sharing, transfer, visualization, querying, updating, information privacy and data source. _____ was originally associated with three key concepts: volume, variety, and velocity. Other concepts later attributed with _____ are veracity and value.

Exam Probability: **High**

55. *Answer choices:*

(see index for correct answer)

- a. Temporal database

- b. Database trigger
- c. Transaction log
- d. Big data

Guidance: level 1

:: Databases ::

A _____ is a repository for persistently storing and managing collections of data which include not just repositories like databases, but also simpler store types such as simple files, emails etc.

Exam Probability: **Medium**

56. *Answer choices:*

(see index for correct answer)

- a. Binary large object
- b. National databases of United States persons
- c. Single-instance storage
- d. Database design

Guidance: level 1

:: Formal methods ::

_____ is the linguistic and philosophical study of meaning, in language, programming languages, formal logics, and semiotics. It is concerned with the relationship between signifiers—like words, phrases, signs, and symbols—and what they stand for in reality, their denotation.

Exam Probability: **High**

57. *Answer choices:*

(see index for correct answer)

- a. State space enumeration
- b. Semantics
- c. Binary moment diagram
- d. Computer-assisted proof

Guidance: level 1

:: Data management ::

_____ is an object-oriented program and library developed by CERN. It was originally designed for particle physics data analysis and contains several features specific to this field, but it is also used in other applications such as astronomy and data mining. The latest release is 6.16.00, as of 2018-11-14.

Exam Probability: **Medium**

58. *Answer choices:*

(see index for correct answer)

- a. Parity file
- b. ROOT
- c. Control break
- d. Tuple

Guidance: level 1

:: Remote sensing ::

_____ is a computer model developed by the University of Idaho, that uses Landsat satellite data to compute and map evapotranspiration . _____ calculates ET as a residual of the surface energy balance, where ET is estimated by keeping account of total net short wave and long wave radiation at the vegetation or soil surface, the amount of heat conducted into soil, and the amount of heat convected into the air above the surface. The difference in these three terms represents the amount of energy absorbed during the conversion of liquid water to vapor, which is ET. _____ expresses near-surface temperature gradients used in heat convection as indexed functions of radio _____ surface temperature, thereby eliminating the need for absolutely accurate surface temperature and the need for air-temperature measurements.

Exam Probability: **Medium**

59. *Answer choices:*

(see index for correct answer)

- a. Ocean Surface Topography Mission

- b. METRIC
- c. Space Saves Society
- d. Orthophoto

Guidance: level 1

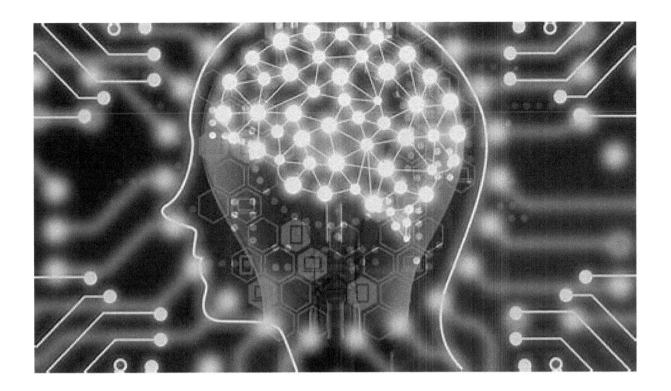

Artificial intelligence

Artificial intelligence, sometimes called machine intelligence, is intelligence demonstrated by machines, in contrast to the natural intelligence displayed by humans and other animals. In computer science AI research is defined as the study of "intelligent agents": any device that perceives its environment and takes actions that maximize its chance of successfully achieving its goals.

:: Automated planning and scheduling ::

In artificial intelligence, _____ denotes a group of techniques for action selection by autonomous agents. These techniques differ from classical planning in two aspects. First, they operate in a timely fashion and hence can cope with highly dynamic and unpredictable environments. Second, they compute just one next action in every instant, based on the current context. Reactive planners often exploit reactive plans, which are stored structures describing the agent's priorities and behaviour.

Exam Probability: **Medium**

1. *Answer choices:*
(see index for correct answer)

- a. Partial-order planning
- b. Automated planning and scheduling
- c. Dynamic Analysis and Replanning Tool
- d. Reactive planning

Guidance: level 1

:: Operating system technology ::

An _____ , for the purposes of chronology and periodization, is an instant in time chosen as the origin of a particular calendar era. The " _____ " serves as a reference point from which time is measured.

Exam Probability: **Low**

2. *Answer choices:*

(see index for correct answer)

- a. Epoch
- b. Operating system abstraction layer
- c. Asynchronous System Trap
- d. Chain loading

Guidance: level 1

:: Machine learning ::

_____ is the machine learning task of learning a function that maps an input to an output based on example input-output pairs. It infers a function from labeled training data consisting of a set of training examples. In _____ , each example is a pair consisting of an input object and a desired output value . A _____ algorithm analyzes the training data and produces an inferred function, which can be used for mapping new examples. An optimal scenario will allow for the algorithm to correctly determine the class labels for unseen instances. This requires the learning algorithm to generalize from the training data to unseen situations in a "reasonable" way .

Exam Probability: **High**

3. *Answer choices:*

(see index for correct answer)

- a. Category utility
- b. Decision rules

- c. Inductive transfer
- d. Bongard problem

Guidance: level 1

:: History of artificial intelligence ::

The _____ was a small informal dining club of young psychiatrists, psychologists, physiologists, mathematicians and engineers who met to discuss issues in cybernetics.

Exam Probability: **Medium**

4. *Answer choices:*

(see index for correct answer)

- a. William Grey Walter
- b. Ratio Club
- c. Intelligent Robotics Group
- d. Information Processing Language

Guidance: level 1

:: Human–computer interaction ::

_____ is an American scientist and artist known for his work with data visualization. Along with Fernanda Viégas, he worked at the Cambridge location of IBM's Thomas J. Watson Research Center as part of the Visual Communication Lab, and created Many Eyes. In April 2010, Wattenberg and Viégas started a new venture called Flowing Media, Inc., to focus on visualization aimed at consumers and mass audiences. Four months later, both of them joined Google as the co-leaders of the Google's "Big Picture" data visualization group in Cambridge, Massachusetts.

Exam Probability: **Low**

5. *Answer choices:*

(see index for correct answer)

- a. Martin M. Wattenberg
- b. Ford Sync
- c. Theraography
- d. Mobile interaction

Guidance: level 1

:: Regression variable selection ::

_____ is the task of selecting a statistical model from a set of candidate models, given data. In the simplest cases, a pre-existing set of data is considered. However, the task can also involve the design of experiments such that the data collected is well-suited to the problem of _____ . Given candidate models of similar predictive or explanatory power, the simplest model is most likely to be the best choice .

6. *Answer choices:*

(see index for correct answer)

- a. Deviance information criterion
- b. Model selection
- c. Focused information criterion
- d. Bayesian information criterion

Guidance: level 1

:: History of artificial intelligence ::

The _____ is the name commonly used for the paper "Artificial Intelligence: A General Survey" by James Lighthill, published in Artificial Intelligence: a paper symposium in 1973.

Exam Probability: **High**

7. *Answer choices:*

(see index for correct answer)

- a. William Grey Walter
- b. AI winter
- c. Blocks world
- d. STUDENT

:: Theoretical computer science ::

A _____ in mathematical logic and computer science is used to define the elements in a set in terms of other elements in the set .

Exam Probability: **Medium**

8. *Answer choices:*

(see index for correct answer)

- a. Recursion
- b. Lowest common ancestor
- c. Nominal techniques
- d. Recursive definition

:: Knowledge representation ::

_____ s or connectionist systems are computing systems vaguely inspired by the biological neural networks and astrocytes that constitute animal brains. The neural network itself is not an algorithm, but rather a framework for many different machine learning algorithms to work together and process complex data inputs. Such systems "learn" to perform tasks by considering examples, generally without being programmed with any task-specific rules. For example, in image recognition, they might learn to identify images that contain cats by analyzing example images that have been manually labeled as "cat" or "no cat" and using the results to identify cats in other images. They do this without any prior knowledge about cats, for example, that they have fur, tails, whiskers and cat-like faces. Instead, they automatically generate identifying characteristics from the learning material that they process.

Exam Probability: **Low**

9. *Answer choices:*

(see index for correct answer)

- a. Reason maintenance
- b. HiLog
- c. Artificial neural network
- d. Visual hierarchy

Guidance: level 1

:: Classification algorithms ::

In computer science, _____ , is a prototype-based supervised classification algorithm. LVQ is the supervised counterpart of vector quantization systems.

Exam Probability: **Low**

10. *Answer choices:*

(see index for correct answer)

- a. Co-training
- b. Learning Vector Quantization
- c. Leptotyphlinae
- d. ALOPEX

Guidance: level 1

:: Time domain analysis ::

In signal processing, the _____ , or _____ function , of a dynamic system is its output when presented with a brief input signal, called an impulse. More generally, an _____ is the reaction of any dynamic system in response to some external change. In both cases, the _____ describes the reaction of the system as a function of time .

Exam Probability: **Medium**

11. *Answer choices:*

(see index for correct answer)

- a. Cross-correlation
- b. Partial autocorrelation function
- c. Impulse response
- d. Time domain

Guidance: level 1

:: Markov models ::

The principle of _____ is formulated for kinetic systems which are decomposed into elementary processes : At equilibrium, each elementary process should be equilibrated by its reverse process.

Exam Probability: **Medium**

12. *Answer choices:*
(see index for correct answer)

- a. GLIMMER
- b. Detailed balance
- c. Hidden Markov model
- d. Population process

Guidance: level 1

:: Classification algorithms ::

_____ , short for Adaptive Boosting, is a machine learning meta-algorithm formulated by Yoav Freund and Robert Schapire, who won the 2003 Gödel Prize for their work. It can be used in conjunction with many other types of learning algorithms to improve performance. The output of the other learning algorithms is combined into a weighted sum that represents the final output of the boosted classifier. _____ is adaptive in the sense that subsequent weak learners are tweaked in favor of those instances misclassified by previous classifiers. _____ is sensitive to noisy data and outliers. In some problems it can be less susceptible to the overfitting problem than other learning algorithms. The individual learners can be weak, but as long as the performance of each one is slightly better than random guessing, the final model can be proven to converge to a strong learner.

Exam Probability: **Low**

13. *Answer choices:*

(see index for correct answer)

- a. AdaBoost
- b. Class membership probabilities
- c. Radial basis function network
- d. Classifier chains

Guidance: level 1

:: Artificial intelligence ::

A _____ is a machine that, like a Turing machine, involves an iteration process that yields a high-quality result, but, whereas a Turing machine uses logic, the _____ uses rounds of variation, selection, and inheritance.

Exam Probability: **Medium**

14. *Answer choices:*

(see index for correct answer)

- a. Cognitive robotics
- b. Fuzzy agent
- c. Epistemic modal logic
- d. AI-complete

Guidance: level 1

:: Unified Modeling Language ::

On 19 July 1926, the Federal Capital Commission commenced operating public bus services between Eastlake in the south and Ainslie in the north.

Exam Probability: **Medium**

15. *Answer choices:*

(see index for correct answer)

- a. Philippe Kruchten
- b. Grady Booch
- c. ACTION
- d. Stereotype

Guidance: level 1

:: Dimension reduction ::

In machine learning, pattern recognition and in image processing, _____ starts from an initial set of measured data and builds derived values intended to be informative and non-redundant, facilitating the subsequent learning and generalization steps, and in some cases leading to better human interpretations. _____ is a dimensionality reduction process, where an initial set of raw variables is reduced to more manageable groups for processing, while still accurately and completely describing the original data set.

Exam Probability: **Low**

16. *Answer choices:*

(see index for correct answer)

- a. Multilinear subspace learning
- b. Sammon mapping
- c. Feature extraction
- d. Sufficient dimension reduction

:: Machine learning ::

Binary or binomial classification is the task of classifying the elements of a given set into two groups on the basis of a classification rule. Contexts requiring a decision as to whether or not an item has some qualitative property, some specified characteristic, or some typical _____ include.

Exam Probability: **Medium**

17. *Answer choices:*

(see index for correct answer)

- a. Semi-supervised learning
- b. Curse of dimensionality
- c. Deep learning
- d. Discriminative model

:: String similarity measures ::

In mathematics, the _____ or Euclidean metric is the "ordinary" straight-line distance between two points in Euclidean space. With this distance, Euclidean space becomes a metric space. The associated norm is called the Euclidean norm. Older literature refers to the metric as the Pythagorean metric. A generalized term for the Euclidean norm is the L2 norm or L2 distance.

Exam Probability: **High**

18. *Answer choices:*

(see index for correct answer)

- a. Euclidean distance
- b. Lee distance
- c. String-to-string correction problem
- d. Hamming distance

Guidance: level 1

:: Theoretical computer science ::

_____ is an area of computer science, cognitive science, and mathematical logic dedicated to understanding different aspects of reasoning. The study of _____ helps produce computer programs that allow computers to reason completely, or nearly completely, automatically. Although _____ is considered a sub-field of artificial intelligence, it also has connections with theoretical computer science, and even philosophy.

19. *Answer choices:*

(see index for correct answer)

- a. Grammar systems theory
- b. ACM SIGACT
- c. Promise theory
- d. Automated reasoning

Guidance: level 1

:: Artificial intelligence ::

A _____ is a class of artificial neural network where connections between nodes form a directed graph along a temporal sequence. This allows it to exhibit temporal dynamic behavior. Unlike feedforward neural networks, RNNs can use their internal state to process sequences of inputs. This makes them applicable to tasks such as unsegmented, connected handwriting recognition or speech recognition.

Exam Probability: **Medium**

20. *Answer choices:*

(see index for correct answer)

- a. Neurorobotics
- b. Constructionist design methodology

- c. Distributed artificial intelligence
- d. Recurrent neural network

Guidance: level 1

:: Knowledge bases ::

A _____ is a technology used to store complex structured and unstructured information used by a computer system. The initial use of the term was in connection with expert systems which were the first knowledge-based systems.

Exam Probability: **Low**

21. *Answer choices:*

(see index for correct answer)

- a. Evi
- b. Freebase
- c. Knowledge base
- d. ThoughtTreasure

Guidance: level 1

:: Graph theory ::

_____ is a numerical measurement of how far apart objects are. In physics or everyday usage, _____ may refer to a physical length or an estimation based on other criteria . In most cases, "_____ from A to B" is interchangeable with "_____ from B to A". In mathematics, a _____ function or metric is a generalization of the concept of physical _____ . A metric is a function that behaves according to a specific set of rules, and is a way of describing what it means for elements of some space to be "close to" or "far away from" each other.

Exam Probability: **Medium**

22. *Answer choices:*

(see index for correct answer)

- a. Icosian calculus
- b. Distance
- c. Vickrey auction
- d. Single-entry single-exit

Guidance: level 1

:: Graphical models ::

_____ , also known as sum-product message passing, is a message-passing algorithm for performing inference on graphical models, such as Bayesian networks and Markov random fields. It calculates the marginal distribution for each unobserved node , conditional on any observed nodes . _____ is commonly used in artificial intelligence and information theory and has demonstrated empirical success in numerous applications including low-density parity-check codes, turbo codes, free energy approximation, and satisfiability.

Exam Probability: **Low**

23. *Answer choices:*

(see index for correct answer)

- a. Belief propagation
- b. Graphical model
- c. Variable elimination
- d. Ancestral graph

Guidance: level 1

:: Data mining ::

In machine learning and pattern recognition, a feature is an individual measurable property or characteristic of a phenomenon being observed. Choosing informative, discriminating and independent features is a crucial step for effective algorithms in pattern recognition, classification and regression. Features are usually numeric, but structural features such as strings and graphs are used in syntactic pattern recognition. The concept of "feature" is related to that of explanatory variable used in statistical techniques such as linear regression.

Exam Probability: **Medium**

24. *Answer choices:*

(see index for correct answer)

- a. Feature vector
- b. Accuracy paradox
- c. Affinity analysis
- d. Structure mining

Guidance: level 1

:: Neural networks ::

_____ is a form of unsupervised learning in artificial neural networks, in which nodes compete for the right to respond to a subset of the input data. A variant of Hebbian learning, _____ works by increasing the specialization of each node in the network. It is well suited to finding clusters within data.

25. *Answer choices:*

(see index for correct answer)

- a. Echo state network
- b. MoneyBee
- c. ADALINE
- d. Phase-of-firing code

Guidance: level 1

:: Automatic identification and data capture ::

_____ or optical character reader, often abbreviated as OCR, is the mechanical or electronic conversion of images of typed, handwritten or printed text into machine-encoded text, whether from a scanned document, a photo of a document, a scene-photo or from subtitle text superimposed on an image .

26. *Answer choices:*

(see index for correct answer)

- a. Label printer
- b. Optical character recognition
- c. Omni-ID

- d. SPARQCode

Guidance: level 1

:: Knowledge representation ::

A _____ is a formalism for knowledge representation. In the first published paper on CGs, John F. Sowa used them to represent the conceptual schemas used in database systems. The first book on CGs applied them to a wide range of topics in artificial intelligence, computer science, and cognitive science.

Exam Probability: **Medium**

27. *Answer choices:*
(see index for correct answer)

- a. Issue trees
- b. Closed world assumption
- c. Conceptual graph
- d. User modeling

Guidance: level 1

:: Artificial intelligence ::

In economics, game theory, decision theory, and artificial intelligence, a _____ is an agent that has clear preferences, models uncertainty via expected values of variables or functions of variables, and always chooses to perform the action with the optimal expected outcome for itself from among all feasible actions. A _____ can be anything that makes decisions, typically a person, firm, machine, or software.

Exam Probability: **High**

28. *Answer choices:*

(see index for correct answer)

- a. Uncanny valley
- b. Diagnosis
- c. Constructionist design methodology
- d. Cognitive robotics

Guidance: level 1

:: Loss functions ::

In statistics, the _____ or mean squared deviation of an estimator measures the average of the squares of the errors—that is, the average squared difference between the estimated values and what is estimated. MSE is a risk function, corresponding to the expected value of the squared error loss. The fact that MSE is almost always strictly positive is because of randomness or because the estimator does not account for information that could produce a more accurate estimate.

29. *Answer choices:*

(see index for correct answer)

- a. Sum of absolute differences
- b. Mean squared error
- c. Huber loss function
- d. Hinge loss

Guidance: level 1

:: Formal methods ::

A _____ is a mathematical model of computation that defines an abstract machine, which manipulates symbols on a strip of tape according to a table of rules. Despite the model's simplicity, given any computer algorithm, a _____ capable of simulating that algorithm's logic can be constructed.

Exam Probability: **High**

30. *Answer choices:*

(see index for correct answer)

- a. DREAM
- b. Turing machine
- c. Logic in computer science

- d. Retrenchment

Guidance: level 1

:: Neural networks ::

_____ , also known as auto-association memory or an autoassociation network, is any type of memory that enables one to retrieve a piece of data from only a tiny sample of itself.

Exam Probability: **Medium**

31. *Answer choices:*

(see index for correct answer)

- a. Autoassociative memory
- b. Biological neural network
- c. Computational neurogenetic modeling
- d. Cortical column

Guidance: level 1

:: Classification algorithms ::

In the field of machine learning, the goal of statistical classification is to use an object's characteristics to identify which class it belongs to. A _____ achieves this by making a classification decision based on the value of a linear combination of the characteristics. An object's characteristics are also known as feature values and are typically presented to the machine in a vector called a feature vector. Such classifiers work well for practical problems such as document classification, and more generally for problems with many variables, reaching accuracy levels comparable to non-_____ s while taking less time to train and use.

Exam Probability: **Medium**

32. *Answer choices:*

(see index for correct answer)

- a. Linear classifier
- b. Nearest centroid classifier
- c. Margin Infused Relaxed Algorithm
- d. Leptotyphlinae

Guidance: level 1

:: Logic in computer science ::

In computer science, GSAT and _____ are local search algorithms to solve Boolean satisfiability problems.

Exam Probability: **Low**

33. *Answer choices:*

(see index for correct answer)

- a. Bunched logic
- b. Event calculus
- c. Unification
- d. Typed lambda calculus

Guidance: level 1

:: Mathematical optimization ::

In mathematical optimization, the method of _____ s is a strategy for finding the local maxima and minima of a function subject to equality constraints . The great advantage of this method is that it allows the optimization to be solved without explicit parameterization in terms of the constraints. As a result, the method of _____ s is widely used to solve challenging constrained optimization problems.

Exam Probability: **High**

34. *Answer choices:*

(see index for correct answer)

- a. Non-linear least squares
- b. Candidate solution
- c. Optimal design
- d. Adaptive projected subgradient method

:: Numerical analysis ::

In mathematics, a _____ is an element of a particular basis for a function space. Every continuous function in the function space can be represented as a linear combination of _____ s, just as every vector in a vector space can be represented as a linear combination of basis vectors.

Exam Probability: **Low**

35. *Answer choices:*

<small>(see index for correct answer)</small>

- a. Smoothed finite element method
- b. Chebyshev nodes
- c. Basis function
- d. Successive parabolic interpolation

:: Dynamical systems ::

_____ s are dynamical systems whose evaluation functions are linear. While dynamical systems, in general, do not have closed-form solutions, _____ s can be solved exactly, and they have a rich set of mathematical properties. Linear systems can also be used to understand the qualitative behavior of general dynamical systems, by calculating the equilibrium points of the system and approximating it as a linear system around each such point.

Exam Probability: **Medium**

36. *Answer choices:*

(see index for correct answer)

- a. Equilibrium point
- b. Linear dynamical system
- c. Wandering set
- d. Superintegrable Hamiltonian system

Guidance: level 1

:: Artificial intelligence ::

_____ is one of the branches of artificial intelligence that is concerned with simulating the human ability to make presumptions about the type and essence of ordinary situations they encounter every day. These assumptions include judgments about the physical properties, purpose, intentions and behavior of people and objects, as well as possible outcomes of their actions and interactions. A device that exhibits _____ will be capable of predicting results and drawing conclusions that are similar to humans' folk psychology and naive physics .

37. *Answer choices:*

(see index for correct answer)

- a. Artificial intelligence marketing
- b. Commonsense reasoning
- c. Artificial psychology
- d. Intelligent word recognition

Guidance: level 1

:: Dynamic programming ::

In information theory, linguistics and computer science, the _____ is a string metric for measuring the difference between two sequences. Informally, the _____ between two words is the minimum number of single-character edits required to change one word into the other. It is named after the Soviet mathematician Vladimir Levenshtein, who considered this distance in 1965.

38. *Answer choices:*

(see index for correct answer)

- a. Viscosity solution
- b. Earley parser

- c. Longest common subsequence problem
- d. Differential dynamic programming

Guidance: level 1

:: Markov models ::

In probability theory, a _____ is a stochastic model used to model randomly changing systems. It is assumed that future states depend only on the current state, not on the events that occurred before it . Generally, this assumption enables reasoning and computation with the model that would otherwise be intractable. For this reason, in the fields of predictive modelling and probabilistic forecasting, it is desirable for a given model to exhibit the Markov property.

Exam Probability: **High**

39. *Answer choices:*

(see index for correct answer)

- a. Burst error
- b. Markov property
- c. Markov switching multifractal
- d. Markov partition

Guidance: level 1

:: Constraint programming ::

In artificial intelligence and operations research, _____ is the process of finding a solution to a set of constraints that impose conditions that the variables must satisfy. A solution is therefore a set of values for the variables that satisfies all constraintsthat is, a point in the feasible region.

Exam Probability: **Low**

40. *Answer choices:*

(see index for correct answer)

- a. AC-3 algorithm
- b. Constraint Composite Graph
- c. Constraint satisfaction
- d. Look-ahead

Guidance: level 1

:: Monte Carlo methods ::

In statistics, _____ is a general technique for estimating properties of a particular distribution, while only having samples generated from a different distribution than the distribution of interest. It is related to umbrella sampling in computational physics. Depending on the application, the term may refer to the process of sampling from this alternative distribution, the process of inference, or both.

41. *Answer choices:*

(see index for correct answer)

- a. Quasi-Monte Carlo method
- b. Coupling from the past
- c. Variance reduction
- d. Auxiliary field Monte Carlo

Guidance: level 1

:: Sensitivity analysis ::

_____ is the study of how the uncertainty in the output of a mathematical model or system can be divided and allocated to different sources of uncertainty in its inputs. A related practice is uncertainty analysis, which has a greater focus on uncertainty quantification and propagation of uncertainty; ideally, uncertainty and _____ should be run in tandem.

42. *Answer choices:*

(see index for correct answer)

- a. Hyperparameter
- b. Elementary effects method

- c. Variance-based sensitivity analysis
- d. Sensitivity analysis

Guidance: level 1

:: Classification algorithms ::

_____ , normal discriminant analysis , or discriminant function analysis is a generalization of Fisher's linear discriminant, a method used in statistics, pattern recognition and machine learning to find a linear combination of features that characterizes or separates two or more classes of objects or events. The resulting combination may be used as a linear classifier, or, more commonly, for dimensionality reduction before later classification.

Exam Probability: **Low**

43. *Answer choices:*

(see index for correct answer)

- a. Linear discriminant analysis
- b. Textual case-based reasoning
- c. Generalization error
- d. Co-training

Guidance: level 1

:: Logic and statistics ::

_____ is a method of statistical inference in which Bayes` theorem is used to update the probability for a hypothesis as more evidence or information becomes available. _____ is an important technique in statistics, and especially in mathematical statistics. Bayesian updating is particularly important in the dynamic analysis of a sequence of data. _____ has found application in a wide range of activities, including science, engineering, philosophy, medicine, sport, and law. In the philosophy of decision theory, _____ is closely related to subjective probability, often called "Bayesian probability".

Exam Probability: **High**

44. *Answer choices:*

(see index for correct answer)

- a. Statistical syllogism
- b. Probabilistic proposition
- c. Epilogism
- d. Statistical proof

Guidance: level 1

:: Classification algorithms ::

In machine learning, support-vector machines are supervised learning models with associated learning algorithms that analyze data used for classification and regression analysis. Given a set of training examples, each marked as belonging to one or the other of two categories, an SVM training algorithm builds a model that assigns new examples to one category or the other, making it a non-probabilistic binary linear classifier. An SVM model is a representation of the examples as points in space, mapped so that the examples of the separate categories are divided by a clear gap that is as wide as possible. New examples are then mapped into that same space and predicted to belong to a category based on which side of the gap they fall.

Exam Probability: **High**

45. *Answer choices:*

(see index for correct answer)

- a. Support vector machine
- b. Novelty detection
- c. IDistance
- d. Quadratic classifier

Guidance: level 1

:: Philosophical methodology ::

In philosophy, _____ is a theory that states that knowledge comes only or primarily from sensory experience. It is one of several views of epistemolgy, the study of human knowledge, along with rationalism and skepticism. _____ emphasises the role of empirical evidence in the formation of ideas, rather than innate ideas or traditions. However, empiricists may argue that traditions arise due to relations of previous sense experiences.

Exam Probability: **Low**

46. *Answer choices:*

(see index for correct answer)

- a. Cartesian doubt
- b. Socratic method
- c. Armchair theorizing
- d. Socratic questioning

Guidance: level 1

:: Decision theory ::

_____ is a negative conscious and emotional reaction to one`s personal decision-making, a choice resulting in action or inaction. _____ is related to perceived opportunity. Its intensity varies over time after the decision, in regard to action versus inaction, and in regard to self-control at a particular age. The self-recrimination which comes with _____ is thought to spur corrective action and adaptation. In Western societies adults have the highest _____ s regarding choices of their education.

47. *Answer choices:*

(see index for correct answer)

- a. Multiscale decision-making
- b. Decision analysis cycle
- c. Regret
- d. Loss aversion

Guidance: level 1

:: Neural networks ::

In neuroscience and computer science, _____ refers to the strength or amplitude of a connection between two nodes, corresponding in biology to the amount of influence the firing of one neuron has on another. The term is typically used in artificial and biological neural network research.

Exam Probability: **Low**

48. *Answer choices:*

(see index for correct answer)

- a. Feedforward neural network
- b. Lernmatrix
- c. Random neural network

- d. Synaptic weight

Guidance: level 1

:: Artificial intelligence ::

In artificial intelligence and cognitive science, the term _____ refers to an agent which is embedded in an environment. The term _____ is commonly used to refer to robots, but some researchers argue that software agents can also be _____ if.

Exam Probability: **High**

49. *Answer choices:*

(see index for correct answer)

- a. Cerebellar Model Articulation Controller
- b. Situated
- c. Unified Theories of Cognition
- d. Legal expert system

Guidance: level 1

:: Web analytics ::

_____ is a web analytics firm. The company is commonly known in the web browser development and technology news communities for its global market share statistics.

50. *Answer choices:*

(see index for correct answer)

- a. WebSideStory
- b. Web audience measurement
- c. Mint
- d. Net Applications

Guidance: level 1

:: History of artificial intelligence ::

Dr. Lawrence Jerome Fogel was a pioneer in evolutionary computation and human factors analysis. He is known as the inventor of active noise cancellation and the father of evolutionary programming. His scientific career spanned nearly six decades and included electrical engineering, aerospace engineering, communication theory, human factors research, information processing, cybernetics, biotechnology, artificial intelligence, and computer science.

51. *Answer choices:*

(see index for correct answer)

- a. Computing Machinery and Intelligence
- b. Lawrence J. Fogel
- c. Intelligent Robotics Group
- d. Johns Hopkins Beast

Guidance: level 1

:: Turing tests ::

The _____ , developed by Alan Turing in 1950, is a test of a machine's ability to exhibit intelligent behaviour equivalent to, or indistinguishable from, that of a human. Turing proposed that a human evaluator would judge natural language conversations between a human and a machine designed to generate human-like responses. The evaluator would be aware that one of the two partners in conversation is a machine, and all participants would be separated from one another. The conversation would be limited to a text-only channel such as a computer keyboard and screen so the result would not depend on the machine's ability to render words as speech. If the evaluator cannot reliably tell the machine from the human, the machine is said to have passed the test. The test results do not depend on the machine's ability to give correct answers to questions, only how closely its answers resemble those a human would give.

Exam Probability: **Medium**

52. *Answer choices:*

(see index for correct answer)

- a. Turing test
- b. Minimum intelligent signal test
- c. Subject matter expert Turing test
- d. Reverse Turing test

Guidance: level 1

:: Logic programming ::

_____ is a type of programming paradigm which is largely based on formal logic. Any program written in a _____ language is a set of sentences in logical form, expressing facts and rules about some problem domain. Major _____ language families include Prolog, answer set programming and Datalog. In all of these languages, rules are written in the form of clauses.

Exam Probability: **High**

53. *Answer choices:*

(see index for correct answer)

- a. SLD resolution
- b. Negation as failure
- c. Functional logic programming
- d. Autoepistemic logic

Guidance: level 1

:: Machine learning algorithms ::

_____ is a model-free reinforcement learning algorithm. The goal of _____ is to learn a policy, which tells an agent what action to take under what circumstances. It does not require a model of the environment, and it can handle problems with stochastic transitions and rewards, without requiring adaptations.

Exam Probability: **Medium**

54. *Answer choices:*

(see index for correct answer)

- a. Genetic Algorithm for Rule Set Production
- b. Q-learning
- c. Quadratic unconstrained binary optimization
- d. Growing self-organizing map

Guidance: level 1

:: Markov networks ::

A _____ is a bipartite graph representing the factorization of a function. In probability theory and its applications, _____ s are used to represent factorization of a probability distribution function, enabling efficient computations, such as the computation of marginal distributions through the sum-product algorithm. One of the important success stories of _____ s and the sum-product algorithm is the decoding of capacity-approaching error-correcting codes, such as LDPC and turbo codes.

Exam Probability: **High**

55. *Answer choices:*

(see index for correct answer)

- a. Markov logic network
- b. Factor graph
- c. Hidden Markov random field

Guidance: level 1

:: Computational science ::

A _____ or simulation experiment is an experiment used to study a computer simulation, also referred to as an in silico system. This area includes computational physics, computational chemistry, computational biology and other similar disciplines.

Exam Probability: **Medium**

56. *Answer choices:*

(see index for correct answer)

- a. Delaunay tessellation field estimator
- b. Lateral computing
- c. Computational mathematics
- d. Computer experiment

Guidance: level 1

:: Search algorithms ::

In computer science, _____ is a heuristic search algorithm that explores a graph by expanding the most promising node in a limited set. _____ is an optimization of best-first search that reduces its memory requirements. Best-first search is a graph search which orders all partial solutions according to some heuristic. But in _____ , only a predetermined number of best partial solutions are kept as candidates. It is thus a greedy algorithm.

Exam Probability: **Medium**

57. *Answer choices:*

(see index for correct answer)

- a. Best bin first
- b. Fibonacci search technique
- c. Linear search

- d. Beam search

Guidance: level 1

:: Data clustering algorithms ::

_____ is a form of clustering in which each data point can belong to more than one cluster.

Exam Probability: **Low**

58. *Answer choices:*
(see index for correct answer)

- a. Spectral clustering
- b. Data stream clustering
- c. Hierarchical clustering
- d. K-means clustering

Guidance: level 1

:: Semantic Web ::

Latent semantic analysis is a technique in natural language processing, in particular distributional semantics, of analyzing relationships between a set of documents and the terms they contain by producing a set of concepts related to the documents and terms. LSA assumes that words that are close in meaning will occur in similar pieces of text . A matrix containing word counts per paragraph is constructed from a large piece of text and a mathematical technique called singular value decomposition is used to reduce the number of rows while preserving the similarity structure among columns. Paragraphs are then compared by taking the cosine of the angle between the two vectors formed by any two columns. Values close to 1 represent very similar paragraphs while values close to 0 represent very dissimilar paragraphs.

Exam Probability: **High**

59. *Answer choices:*

(see index for correct answer)

- a. Semantic Web Services
- b. Cwm
- c. ISO 15926
- d. Latent semantic indexing

Guidance: level 1

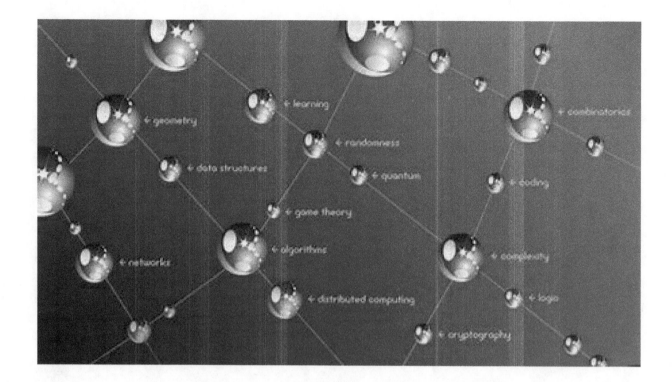

Computer networking

A computer network, or data network, is a digital telecommunications network which allows nodes to share resources. In computer networks, computing devices exchange data with each other using connections (data links) between nodes. These data links are established over cable media such as wires or optic cables, or wireless media such as WiFi.

:: Control characters ::

_____ is the boundless three-dimensional extent in which objects and events have relative position and direction. Physical _____ is often conceived in three linear dimensions, although modern physicists usually consider it, with time, to be part of a boundless four-dimensional continuum known as _____ time. The concept of _____ is considered to be of fundamental importance to an understanding of the physical universe. However, disagreement continues between philosophers over whether it is itself an entity, a relationship between entities, or part of a conceptual framework.

Exam Probability: **Low**

1. *Answer choices:*

(see index for correct answer)

- a. Bell character
- b. Combining Grapheme Joiner
- c. Space
- d. Escape character

Guidance: level 1

:: Computer access control ::

_____ is the act of confirming the truth of an attribute of a single piece of data claimed true by an entity. In contrast with identification, which refers to the act of stating or otherwise indicating a claim purportedly attesting to a person or thing's identity, _____ is the process of actually confirming that identity. It might involve confirming the identity of a person by validating their identity documents, verifying the authenticity of a website with a digital certificate, determining the age of an artifact by carbon dating, or ensuring that a product is what its packaging and labeling claim to be. In other words, _____ often involves verifying the validity of at least one form of identification.

Exam Probability: **High**

2. *Answer choices:*

(see index for correct answer)

- a. Directory service
- b. Richacls
- c. Authentication
- d. MicroID

Guidance: level 1

:: Mathematical logic ::

_____ is an arrangement and organization of interrelated elements in a material object or system, or the object or system so organized. Material _____ s include man-made objects such as buildings and machines and natural objects such as biological organisms, minerals and chemicals. Abstract _____ s include data _____ s in computer science and musical form. Types of _____ include a hierarchy , a network featuring many-to-many links, or a lattice featuring connections between components that are neighbors in space.

Exam Probability: **Low**

3. *Answer choices:*

(see index for correct answer)

- a. Structure
- b. T-schema
- c. Elementary definition
- d. Characteristic sequence

Guidance: level 1

:: Computer networking ::

A backbone is a part of computer network that interconnects various pieces of network, providing a path for the exchange of information between different LANs or subnetworks. A backbone can tie together diverse networks in the same building, in different buildings in a campus environment, or over wide areas. Normally, the backbone's capacity is greater than the networks connected to it.

4. *Answer choices:*

(see index for correct answer)

- a. Backbone network
- b. Content delivery network
- c. Computer network diagram
- d. Sublayer

Guidance: level 1

:: Radio resource management ::

A _____ or mobile network is a communication network where the last link is wireless. The network is distributed over land areas called cells, each served by at least one fixed-location transceiver, but more normally three cell sites or base transceiver stations. These base stations provide the cell with the network coverage which can be used for transmission of voice, data, and other types of content. A cell typically uses a different set of frequencies from neighbouring cells, to avoid interference and provide guaranteed service quality within each cell.

Exam Probability: **Low**

5. *Answer choices:*

(see index for correct answer)

- a. Cellular network
- b. Cooperative diversity
- c. Precoding
- d. Hierarchical modulation

Guidance: level 1

:: Network architecture ::

_____ is "the concept of interconnecting different types of networks to build a large, global network" such that any pair of connected hosts can exchange packets. To build an internetwork, the following are needed: A standardized scheme to address packets to any host on any participating network; a standardized protocol defining format and handling of transmitted packets; components interconnecting the participating networks by routing packets to their destinations based on standardized addresses.

Exam Probability: **High**

6. *Answer choices:*

(see index for correct answer)

- a. Internetworking
- b. Optical mesh network
- c. Network address
- d. Fiber to the x

Guidance: level 1

:: Application layer protocols ::

The _____ is a network management protocol used on UDP/IP networks whereby a DHCP server dynamically assigns an IP address and other network configuration parameters to each device on a network so they can communicate with other IP networks. A DHCP server enables computers to request IP addresses and networking parameters automatically from the Internet service provider , reducing the need for a network administrator or a user to manually assign IP addresses to all network devices. In the absence of a DHCP server, a computer or other device on the network needs to be manually assigned an IP address, or to assign itself an APIPA address, which will not enable it to communicate outside its local subnet.

Exam Probability: **Medium**

7. *Answer choices:*

(see index for correct answer)

- a. Message send protocol
- b. Media Resource Control Protocol
- c. Real Time Streaming Protocol
- d. Dynamic Host Configuration Protocol

Guidance: level 1

:: Internet Protocol ::

The _____ is a group of internetworking methods, protocols, and specifications in the Internet protocol suite that are used to transport network packets from the originating host across network boundaries, if necessary, to the destination host specified by an IP address. The _____ derives its name from its function facilitating internetworking, which is the concept of connecting multiple networks with each other through gateways.

Exam Probability: **Low**

8. *Answer choices:*

(see index for correct answer)

- a. IP Network Transformation
- b. Access network discovery and selection function
- c. Group Destination Address
- d. Internet layer

Guidance: level 1

:: Compiler construction ::

In computer science, the _____ of data is its structure described as a data type , independent of any particular representation or encoding. This is particularly used in the representation of text in computer languages, which are generally stored in a tree structure as an _____ tree. _____ , which only consists of the structure of data, is contrasted with concrete syntax, which also includes information about the representation. For example, concrete syntax includes features like parentheses or commas which are not included in the _____ , as they are implicit in the structure.

9. *Answer choices:*

(see index for correct answer)

- a. Abstract syntax
- b. compile-time
- c. Metacompilation
- d. Semantic dictionary encoding

Guidance: level 1

:: Personal area networks ::

A _____ is a computer network for interconnecting devices centered on an individual person's workspace. A PAN provides data transmission among devices such as computers, smartphones, tablets and personal digital assistants. PANs can be used for communication among the personal devices themselves, or for connecting to a higher level network and the Internet where one master device takes up the role as gateway. A PAN may be wireless or carried over wired interfaces such as USB.

10. *Answer choices:*

(see index for correct answer)

- a. Daintree Networks

- b. Ember
- c. IEEE 1394
- d. Personal area network

Guidance: level 1

:: Network topology ::

A _____ is a network topology in which each node connects to exactly two other nodes, forming a single continuous pathway for signals through each node - a ring. Data travels from node to node, with each node along the way handling every packet.

Exam Probability: **Medium**

11. *Answer choices:*

(see index for correct answer)

- a. Mesh node
- b. Shared mesh
- c. Network topology
- d. Ring network

Guidance: level 1

:: Transport layer protocols ::

In computer networking, the _____ is one of the core members of the Internet protocol suite. The protocol was designed by David P. Reed in 1980 and formally defined in RFC 768. With UDP, computer applications can send messages, in this case referred to as datagrams, to other hosts on an Internet Protocol network. Prior communications are not required in order to set up communication channels or data paths.

Exam Probability: **High**

12. *Answer choices:*

(see index for correct answer)

- a. UDP Lite
- b. ALCAP
- c. User Datagram Protocol
- d. Reliable User Datagram Protocol

Guidance: level 1

:: Unified Modeling Language ::

On 19 July 1926, the Federal Capital Commission commenced operating public bus services between Eastlake in the south and Ainslie in the north.

Exam Probability: **Low**

13. *Answer choices:*

(see index for correct answer)

- a. Enterprise Distributed Object Computing
- b. Model-driven architecture
- c. Swim lane
- d. Action

Guidance: level 1

:: Radio modulation modes ::

_____ is the name of a family of digital modulation methods and a related family of analog modulation methods widely used in modern telecommunications to transmit information. It conveys two analog message signals, or two digital bit streams, by changing the amplitudes of two carrier waves, using the amplitude-shift keying digital modulation scheme or amplitude modulation analog modulation scheme. The two carrier waves of the same frequency are out of phase with each other by 90°, a condition known as orthogonality and as quadrature. Being the same frequency, the modulated carriers add together, but can be coherently separated because of their orthogonality property. Another key property is that the modulations are low-frequency/low-bandwidth waveforms compared to the carrier frequency, which is known as the narrowband assumption.

Exam Probability: **Medium**

14. *Answer choices:*

(see index for correct answer)

- a. Carrier shift

- b. Angle modulation
- c. Amplitude modulation
- d. Chirp spread spectrum

Guidance: level 1

:: Computer access control ::

In computing, _____ or name service maps the names of network resources to their respective network addresses. It is a shared information infrastructure for locating, managing, administering and organizing everyday items and network resources, which can include volumes, folders, files, printers, users, groups, devices, telephone numbers and other objects. A _____ is a critical component of a network operating system. A directory server or name server is a server which provides such a service. Each resource on the network is considered an object by the directory server. Information about a particular resource is stored as a collection of attributes associated with that resource or object.

Exam Probability: **Low**

15. *Answer choices:*

(see index for correct answer)

- a. Federated identity
- b. Role hierarchy
- c. Security question
- d. Database audit

:: Internet architecture ::

In computer networking, IntServ or _____ is an architecture that specifies the elements to guarantee quality of service on networks. IntServ can for example be used to allow video and sound to reach the receiver without interruption.

Exam Probability: **Medium**

16. *Answer choices:*

(see index for correct answer)

- a. DIMES
- b. Time to live
- c. IP fragmentation
- d. Core router

:: Web development ::

A _____ is server software, or hardware dedicated to running said software, that can satisfy World Wide Web client requests. A _____ can, in general, contain one or more websites. A _____ processes incoming network requests over HTTP and several other related protocols.

Exam Probability: **Low**

17. *Answer choices:*

(see index for correct answer)

- a. Panorama viewer
- b. Conversion path
- c. Bookmarklet
- d. Static web page

Guidance: level 1

:: Denial-of-service attacks ::

In computing, a _____ is a cyber-attack in which the perpetrator seeks to make a machine or network resource unavailable to its intended users by temporarily or indefinitely disrupting services of a host connected to the Internet. Denial of service is typically accomplished by flooding the targeted machine or resource with superfluous requests in an attempt to overload systems and prevent some or all legitimate requests from being fulfilled.

Exam Probability: **Low**

18. *Answer choices:*

(see index for correct answer)

- a. Ping of death
- b. Alexander Petrov
- c. Denial-of-service attack
- d. UDP Unicorn

Guidance: level 1

:: Malware ::

The _____ is a story from the Trojan War about the subterfuge that the Greeks used to enter the independent city of Troy and win the war. In the canonical version, after a fruitless 10-year siege, the Greeks constructed a huge wooden horse, and hid a select force of men inside including Odysseus. The Greeks pretended to sail away, and the Trojans pulled the horse into their city as a victory trophy. That night the Greek force crept out of the horse and opened the gates for the rest of the Greek army, which had sailed back under cover of night. The Greeks entered and destroyed the city of Troy, ending the war.

Exam Probability: **High**

19. *Answer choices:*

(see index for correct answer)

- a. Mobile code
- b. Hover ad

- c. Trojan horse
- d. Flame

Guidance: level 1

:: World Wide Web ::

The _____ is an application protocol for distributed, collaborative, hypermedia information systems. HTTP is the foundation of data communication for the World Wide Web, where hypertext documents include hyperlinks to other resources that the user can easily access, for example by a mouse click or by tapping the screen in a web browser. HTTP was developed to facilitate hypertext and the World Wide Web.

Exam Probability: **Medium**

20. *Answer choices:*

(see index for correct answer)

- a. Stanford Web Credibility Project
- b. Hypertext Transfer Protocol
- c. Ovi
- d. Open Web

Guidance: level 1

:: Application layer protocols ::

_____ is a cryptographic network protocol for operating network services securely over an unsecured network. Typical applications include remote command-line login and remote command execution, but any network service can be secured with SSH.

Exam Probability: **High**

21. *Answer choices:*

(see index for correct answer)

- a. NETCONF
- b. 3G-324M
- c. Internet Message Access Protocol
- d. Remote Desktop Protocol

Guidance: level 1

:: File sharing networks ::

_____ computing or networking is a distributed application architecture that partitions tasks or workloads between peers. Peers are equally privileged, equipotent participants in the application. They are said to form a _____ network of nodes.

Exam Probability: **Low**

22. *Answer choices:*

(see index for correct answer)

- a. Gnutella
- b. Wirehog
- c. WASTE
- d. Peer-to-peer

Guidance: level 1

:: Internet architecture ::

In computer networking a _____ , or routing information base , is a data table stored in a router or a networked computer that lists the routes to particular network destinations, and in some cases, metrics associated with those routes. The _____ contains information about the topology of the network immediately around it. The construction of _____ s is the primary goal of routing protocols. Static routes are entries made in a _____ by non-automatic means and which are fixed rather than being the result of some network topology "discovery" procedure.

Exam Probability: **Medium**

23. *Answer choices:*
(see index for correct answer)

- a. Peering
- b. Internet backbone
- c. Global network positioning

- d. Semaphore Flag Signaling System

Guidance: level 1

:: Mathematical structures ::

_____ s serve several societal needs – primarily as shelter from weather, security, living space, privacy, to store belongings, and to comfortably live and work. A _____ as a shelter represents a physical division of the human habitat and the outside .

Exam Probability: **Low**

24. *Answer choices:*
(see index for correct answer)

- a. Ideal ring bundle
- b. Weakly o-minimal structure
- c. Building
- d. Periodic matrix set

Guidance: level 1

:: Wireless networking ::

_____ communication, or sometimes simply _____ , is the transfer of information or power between two or more points that are not connected by an electrical conductor. The most common _____ technologies use radio waves. With radio waves distances can be short, such as a few meters for Bluetooth or as far as millions of kilometers for deep-space radio communications. It encompasses various types of fixed, mobile, and portable applications, including two-way radios, cellular telephones, personal digital assistants , and _____ networking. Other examples of applications of radio _____ technology include GPS units, garage door openers, _____ computer mice, keyboards and headsets, headphones, radio receivers, satellite television, broadcast television and cordless telephones. Somewhat less common methods of achieving _____ communications include the use of other electromagnetic _____ technologies, such as light, magnetic, or electric fields or the use of sound.

Exam Probability: **Medium**

25. *Answer choices:*

(see index for correct answer)

- a. Multipoint relay
- b. Wireless
- c. Toothing
- d. Negroponte switch

Guidance: level 1

:: Internet protocols ::

The _____ is one of the oldest distance-vector routing protocols which employ the hop count as a routing metric. RIP prevents routing loops by implementing a limit on the number of hops allowed in a path from source to destination. The largest number of hops allowed for RIP is 15, which limits the size of networks that RIP can support.

Exam Probability: **Low**

26. *Answer choices:*

(see index for correct answer)

- a. LISTSERV
- b. M3UA
- c. Extensible Name Service
- d. Routing Information Protocol

Guidance: level 1

:: Computer networking ::

_____ is a technique of network relaying to overcome the problems perceived by traditional IP-table switching . Here, the switching of network packets occurs at a lower level, namely the data link layer rather than the traditional network layer.

Exam Probability: **Medium**

27. *Answer choices:*

(see index for correct answer)

- a. Traffic flow
- b. Associative browsing
- c. Application Session Controller
- d. Timing channel

Guidance: level 1

:: Network addressing ::

In the Internet addressing architecture, a _____ is a network that uses private IP address space. Both, the IPv4 and the IPv6 specifications define private addressing ranges. These addresses are commonly used for local area networks in residential, office, and enterprise environments. Private IP address spaces were originally defined in an effort to delay IPv4 address exhaustion.

Exam Probability: **Low**

28. *Answer choices:*

(see index for correct answer)

- a. Dot-decimal notation
- b. Multicast address
- c. Host address
- d. Private network

:: Network addressing ::

A media access control address of a device is a unique identifier assigned to a network interface controller . For communications within a network segment, it is used as a network address for most IEEE 802 network technologies, including Ethernet, Wi-Fi, and Bluetooth. Within the Open Systems Interconnection model, _____ es are used in the medium access control protocol sublayer of the data link layer. As typically represented, _____ es are recognizable as six groups of two hexadecimal digits, separated by hyphens, colons, or no separator.

Exam Probability: **Medium**

29. *Answer choices:*

<small>(see index for correct answer)</small>

- a. Circuit ID
- b. Provider-aggregatable address space
- c. Multicast address
- d. Organizationally unique identifier

:: Computer security ::

In the fields of physical security and information security, _____ is the selective restriction of access to a place or other resource. The act of accessing may mean consuming, entering, or using. Permission to access a resource is called authorization.

Exam Probability: **Medium**

30. *Answer choices:*

(see index for correct answer)

- a. Event data
- b. Trust boundary
- c. Economics of security
- d. Access control

Guidance: level 1

:: Domain name system ::

A _____ is a computer application that implements a network service for providing responses to queries against a directory service. It translates an often humanly meaningful, text-based identifier to a system-internal, often numeric identification or addressing component. This service is performed by the server in response to a service protocol request.

Exam Probability: **High**

31. *Answer choices:*

(see index for correct answer)

- a. Wildcard DNS record
- b. Domain name speculation
- c. OpenDNSSEC
- d. Domain name registry

Guidance: level 1

:: Formal languages ::

A _____ is a mark, sign or word that indicates, signifies, or is understood as representing an idea, object, or relationship. _____ s allow people to go beyond what is known or seen by creating linkages between otherwise very different concepts and experiences. All communication is achieved through the use of _____ s. _____ s take the form of words, sounds, gestures, ideas or visual images and are used to convey other ideas and beliefs. For example, a red octagon may be a _____ for "STOP". On a map, a blue line might represent a river. Numerals are _____ s for numbers. Alphabetic letters may be _____ s for sounds. Personal names are _____ s representing individuals. A red rose may _____ ize love and compassion. The variable `x`, in a mathematical equation, may _____ ize the position of a particle in space.

Exam Probability: **Low**

32. *Answer choices:*

(see index for correct answer)

- a. Rational language
- b. Post canonical system
- c. Shortest common supersequence
- d. Locally catenative sequence

Guidance: level 1

:: Network management ::

In network management, _____ is the set of functions that detect, isolate, and correct malfunctions in a telecommunications network, compensate for environmental changes, and include maintaining and examining error logs, accepting and acting on error detection notifications, tracing and identifying faults, carrying out sequences of diagnostics tests, correcting faults, reporting error conditions, and localizing and tracing faults by examining and manipulating database information.

Exam Probability: **Low**

33. *Answer choices:*

(see index for correct answer)

- a. Telecommunication Management Network model
- b. Bipartite network projection
- c. Network-to-network interface
- d. Fault management

Guidance: level 1

:: Metropolitan area networks ::

A metropolitan-area Ethernet, Ethernet MAN, or _____ network is a metropolitan area network that is based on Ethernet standards. It is commonly used to connect subscribers to a larger service network or the Internet. Businesses can also use metropolitan-area Ethernet to connect their own offices to each other.

Exam Probability: **High**

34. *Answer choices:*

(see index for correct answer)

- a. Motorola Canopy
- b. Gigabit Chicago
- c. Metro Ethernet
- d. WiMAX

Guidance: level 1

:: Network architecture ::

A _____ is a logical division of a computer network, in which all nodes can reach each other by broadcast at the data link layer. A _____ can be within the same LAN segment or it can be bridged to other LAN segments.

35. *Answer choices:*

(see index for correct answer)

- a. Interconnection
- b. Medium Dependent Interface
- c. Broadcast domain
- d. Channel bonding

Guidance: level 1

:: MPLS networking ::

_____ is a routing technique in telecommunications networks that directs data from one node to the next based on short path labels rather than long network addresses, thus avoiding complex lookups in a routing table and speeding traffic flows. The labels identify virtual links between distant nodes rather than endpoints. MPLS can encapsulate packets of various network protocols, hence the "multiprotocol" reference on its name. MPLS supports a range of access technologies, including T1/E1, ATM, Frame Relay, and DSL.

Exam Probability: **High**

36. *Answer choices:*

(see index for correct answer)

- a. Forwarding equivalence class

- b. Multiprotocol Label Switching
- c. P Router
- d. Virtual Leased Line

Guidance: level 1

:: BIOS ::

_____ Ltd is an American company that designs, develops and supports core system software for personal computers and other computing devices. The company's products commonly referred to as BIOS or firmware support and enable the compatibility, connectivity, security and management of the various components and technologies used in such devices. _____ and IBM developed the El Torito standard.

Exam Probability: **Medium**

37. *Answer choices:*

(see index for correct answer)

- a. Phoenix Technologies
- b. Extended System Configuration Data
- c. MBRwizard
- d. BIOS Boot partition

Guidance: level 1

:: Network protocols ::

A _____ is a means of transporting data over a packet switched
computer network in such a way that it appears as though there is a dedicated
physical layer link between the source and destination end systems of this
data. The term _____ is synonymous with virtual connection and virtual
channel. Before a connection or _____ may be used, it has to be
established, between two or more nodes or software applications, by configuring
the relevant parts of the interconnecting network. After that, a bit stream or
byte stream may be delivered between the nodes; hence, a _____ protocol
allows higher level protocols to avoid dealing with the division of data into
segments, packets, or frames.

Exam Probability: **Low**

38. *Answer choices:*

(see index for correct answer)

- a. AppleTalk
- b. RP-570
- c. Synchronous Ethernet
- d. Synchronous optical networking

Guidance: level 1

:: Network protocols ::

PIP in telecommunications and datacommunications stands for Private Internet Protocol or _____ . PIP refers to connectivity into a private extranet network which by its design emulates the functioning of the Internet. Specifically, the Internet uses a routing protocol called border gateway protocol , as do most multiprotocol label switching networks. With this design, there is an ambiguity to the route that a packet can take while traversing the network. Wherein the Internet is a public offering, MPLS PIP networks are private. This lends a known, often used, and comfortable network design model for private implementation.

Exam Probability: **Medium**

39. *Answer choices:*

(see index for correct answer)

- a. DMX512
- b. Communications protocol
- c. Transport Driver Interface
- d. Private IP

Guidance: level 1

:: History of the Internet ::

The _____ is an American nonprofit organization founded in 1992 to provide leadership in Internet-related standards, education, access, and policy. Its mission is "to promote the open development, evolution and use of the Internet for the benefit of all people throughout the world".

40. *Answer choices:*

(see index for correct answer)

- a. Internet Society
- b. CERN httpd
- c. Stanford Digital Library Project
- d. Dave Raggett

Guidance: level 1

:: Network management ::

_____ is the process of administering and managing computer networks. Services provided by this discipline include fault analysis, performance management, provisioning of networks and maintaining the quality of service. Software that enables network administrators to perform their functions is called _____ software.

Exam Probability: **Medium**

41. *Answer choices:*

(see index for correct answer)

- a. In-band signaling
- b. Active monitor

- c. Management agent
- d. Network management

Guidance: level 1

:: Domain name system ::

Within the Internet, _____ s are formed by the rules and procedures of the _____ System . Any name registered in the DNS is a _____ . _____ s are used in various networking contexts and for application-specific naming and addressing purposes. In general, a _____ represents an Internet Protocol resource, such as a personal computer used to access the Internet, a server computer hosting a web site, or the web site itself or any other service communicated via the Internet. In 2017, 330.6 million _____ s had been registered.

Exam Probability: **Low**

42. *Answer choices:*

(see index for correct answer)

- a. Gauss Research Laboratory
- b. Domain name
- c. TSIG
- d. .local

Guidance: level 1

:: Internet architecture ::

_____ is a method of remapping one IP address space into another by modifying network address information in the IP header of packets while they are in transit across a traffic routing device. The technique was originally used as a shortcut to avoid the need to readdress every host when a network was moved. It has become a popular and essential tool in conserving global address space in the face of IPv4 address exhaustion. One Internet-routable IP address of a NAT gateway can be used for an entire private network.

Exam Probability: **Low**

43. *Answer choices:*

(see index for correct answer)

- a. Future Internet Research and Experimentation
- b. Network Load Balancing
- c. Sorcerer%27s Apprentice Syndrome
- d. Information transfer node

Guidance: level 1

:: Local area networks ::

_____ local area network technology is a communications protocol for local area networks. It uses a special three-byte frame called a "token" that travels around a logical "ring" of workstations or servers. This token passing is a channel access method providing fair access for all stations, and eliminating the collisions of contention-based access methods.

Exam Probability: **Medium**

44. *Answer choices:*

(see index for correct answer)

- a. Token ring
- b. Chaosnet
- c. PhoneNet
- d. Local area network

Guidance: level 1

:: Network performance ::

_____ is a bandwidth management technique used on computer networks which delays some or all datagrams to bring them into compliance with a desired traffic profile. _____ is used to optimize or guarantee performance, improve latency, or increase usable bandwidth for some kinds of packets by delaying other kinds. It is often confused with traffic policing, the distinct but related practice of packet dropping and packet marking.

Exam Probability: **High**

- a. Throughput
- b. NetEqualizer
- c. Tacit Networks
- d. Bandwidth management

:: Internet architecture ::

In networking jargon, the computers that are connected to a computer network are sometimes referred to as _____ s or end stations. They are labeled _____ s because they sit at the edge of the network. The end user always interacts with the _____ s. _____ s are the devices that provide information or services.

Exam Probability: **Low**

- a. supernet
- b. End system
- c. Last mile
- d. classful

:: Internet architecture ::

_____ is defined as that aspect of Internet network engineering dealing with the issue of performance evaluation and performance optimization of operational IP networks. Traffic engineering encompasses the application of technology and scientific principles to the measurement, characterization, modeling, and control of Internet traffic [RFC-2702, AWD2].

Exam Probability: **High**

47. *Answer choices:*

(see index for correct answer)

- a. Internet traffic engineering
- b. Clean Slate Program
- c. Supernetwork
- d. Localhost

:: Transmission Control Protocol ::

The _____ is one of the main protocols of the Internet protocol suite. It originated in the initial network implementation in which it complemented the Internet Protocol . Therefore, the entire suite is commonly referred to as TCP/IP. TCP provides reliable, ordered, and error-checked delivery of a stream of octets between applications running on hosts communicating via an IP network. Major internet applications such as the World Wide Web, email, remote administration, and file transfer rely on TCP. Applications that do not require reliable data stream service may use the User Datagram Protocol , which provides a connectionless datagram service that emphasizes reduced latency over reliability.

Exam Probability: **Medium**

48. *Answer choices:*

(see index for correct answer)

- a. TCP congestion-avoidance algorithm
- b. TCP Fast Open
- c. Slow-start
- d. Transmission Control Protocol

Guidance: level 1

:: Fibre Channel ::

_____ is a high-speed data transfer protocol providing in-order, lossless delivery of raw block data, primarily used to connect computer data storage to servers. _____ is mainly used in storage area networks in commercial data centers. _____ networks form a switched fabric because they operate in unison as one big switch. _____ typically runs on optical fiber cables within and between data centers, but can also run on copper cabling.

Exam Probability: **Medium**

49. *Answer choices:*

(see index for correct answer)

- a. NPIV
- b. Fibre Channel
- c. Fibre Channel switch
- d. Fibre Channel zoning

Guidance: level 1

:: Local area networks ::

A _____ is any broadcast domain that is partitioned and isolated in a computer network at the data link layer . LAN is the abbreviation for local area network and in this context virtual refers to a physical object recreated and altered by additional logic. VLANs work by applying tags to network frames and handling these tags in networking systems – creating the appearance and functionality of network traffic that is physically on a single network but acts as if it is split between separate networks. In this way, VLANs can keep network applications separate despite being connected to the same physical network, and without requiring multiple sets of cabling and networking devices to be deployed.

Exam Probability: **Medium**

50. *Answer choices:*

(see index for correct answer)

- a. Virtual LAN
- b. Serial over LAN
- c. Village Area Network
- d. PhoneNet

Guidance: level 1

:: Cryptography ::

_____ or cryptology is the practice and study of techniques for secure communication in the presence of third parties called adversaries. More generally, _____ is about constructing and analyzing protocols that prevent third parties or the public from reading private messages; various aspects in information security such as data confidentiality, data integrity, authentication, and non-repudiation are central to modern _____. Modern _____ exists at the intersection of the disciplines of mathematics, computer science, electrical engineering, communication science, and physics. Applications of _____ include electronic commerce, chip-based payment cards, digital currencies, computer passwords, and military communications.

Exam Probability: **Low**

51. *Answer choices:*

(see index for correct answer)

- a. Salt
- b. Trapdoor function
- c. Server-based signatures
- d. Self-shrinking generator

Guidance: level 1

:: Networking hardware ::

A _____ , patch bay, patch field or jack field is a device or unit featuring a number of jacks, usually of the same or similar type, for the use of connecting and routing circuits for monitoring, interconnecting, and testing circuits in a convenient, flexible manner. _____ s are commonly used in computer networking, recording studios, radio and television.

Exam Probability: **Medium**

52. *Answer choices:*

(see index for correct answer)

- a. DECserver
- b. Network processor
- c. Patch panel
- d. PACX

Guidance: level 1

:: System administration ::

A _____ is a system monitor program used to provide information about the processes and applications running on a computer, as well as the general status of the computer. Some implementations can also be used to terminate processes and applications, as well as change the processes` scheduling priority. In some environments, users can access a _____ with the Control-Alt-Delete keyboard shortcut.

Exam Probability: **Medium**

53. *Answer choices:*

(see index for correct answer)

- a. Conky
- b. Iostat
- c. Task manager
- d. Tivoli Management Framework

Guidance: level 1

:: Application layer protocols ::

The _____ is a communication protocol for electronic mail transmission. As an Internet standard, SMTP was first defined in 1982 by RFC 821, and updated in 2008 by RFC 5321 to Extended SMTP additions, which is the protocol variety in widespread use today. Mail servers and other message transfer agents use SMTP to send and receive mail messages. Proprietary systems such as Microsoft Exchange and IBM Notes and webmail systems such as Outlook.com, Gmail and Yahoo! Mail may use non-standard protocols internally, but all use SMTP when sending to or receiving email from outside their own systems. SMTP servers commonly use the Transmission Control Protocol on port number 25.

Exam Probability: **Medium**

54. *Answer choices:*

(see index for correct answer)

- a. Message Session Relay Protocol

- b. CAMEL Application Part
- c. X.400
- d. X-Video Bitstream Acceleration

Guidance: level 1

:: Digital circuits ::

_____ is the length of time taken for the quantity of interest to reach its destination. It can relate to networking, electronics or physics.

Exam Probability: **High**

55. *Answer choices:*

(see index for correct answer)

- a. Propagation delay
- b. Open collector
- c. Address decoder
- d. Multivibrator

Guidance: level 1

:: Command shells ::

CMD, cmd or cmd.exe , also known as _____ , is the command-line interpreter in the OS/2, eComStation, Windows NT, Windows CE, and ReactOS operating systems. It is the counterpart of COMMAND.COM in DOS and Windows 9x systems, and analogous to the Unix shells used on Unix-like systems. The initial version of cmd.exe for Windows NT was developed by Therese Stowell.

Exam Probability: **Medium**

56. *Answer choices:*

(see index for correct answer)

- a. Restricted shell
- b. Conversational Monitor System
- c. DIGITAL Command Language
- d. COMMAND.COM

Guidance: level 1

:: Servers (computing) ::

In computing, a _____ is a computer attached to a network that provides a location for shared disk access, i.e. shared storage of computer files that can be accessed by the workstations that are able to reach the computer that shares the access through a computer network. The term server highlights the role of the machine in the client–server scheme, where the clients are the workstations using the storage. It is common that a _____ does not perform computational tasks, and does not run programs on behalf of its clients.It is designed primarily to enable the storage and retrieval of data while the computation is carried out by the workstations.

57. *Answer choices:*

(see index for correct answer)

- a. Mobile Server
- b. File server
- c. Redundant Array of Inexpensive Servers
- d. Communications server

Guidance: level 1

:: Internet architecture ::

_____ is the description or measurement of the overall performance of a service, such as a telephony or computer network or a cloud computing service, particularly the performance seen by the users of the network. To quantitatively measure _____ , several related aspects of the network service are often considered, such as packet loss, bit rate, throughput, transmission delay, availability, jitter, etc.

Exam Probability: **High**

58. *Answer choices:*

(see index for correct answer)

- a. Quality of service
- b. Herbert Van de Sompel

- c. Time to live
- d. Border Gateway Multicast Protocol

Guidance: level 1

:: Fiber optics ::

An _____ is a flexible, transparent fiber made by drawing glass or plastic to a diameter slightly thicker than that of a human hair. _____ s are used most often as a means to transmit light between the two ends of the fiber and find wide usage in fiber-optic communications, where they permit transmission over longer distances and at higher bandwidths than electrical cables. Fibers are used instead of metal wires because signals travel along them with less loss; in addition, fibers are immune to electromagnetic interference, a problem from which metal wires suffer excessively. Fibers are also used for illumination and imaging, and are often wrapped in bundles so they may be used to carry light into, or images out of confined spaces, as in the case of a fiberscope. Specially designed fibers are also used for a variety of other applications, some of them being fiber optic sensors and fiber lasers.

Exam Probability: **Medium**

59. *Answer choices:*

(see index for correct answer)

- a. Distributed temperature sensing
- b. Cleave
- c. Narinder Singh Kapany
- d. Fiber optic sensor

INDEX: Correct Answers

Foundations of Computer Science

1. d: Symbol

2. d: Mail

3. a: Music

4. c: Window

5. d: Task manager

6. d: Document

7. a: Volatile memory

8. b: World Wide Web

9. d: Pseudocode

10. d: Network administrator

11. : Cloud computing

12. a: Executable

13. d: Analytical Engine

14. a: Structure

15. b: File Transfer Protocol

16. : Unicode

17. d: Name

18. : FORMAT

19. b: Markup language

20. a: Network architecture

21. b: Mac OS

22. b: Grid computing

23. : Pop-up ad

24. d: Desktop publishing

25. a: Virtual reality

26. d: Personal firewall

27. d: ROOT

28. : Online community

29. a: Communications protocol

30. c: Adobe Photoshop

31. : Telephone call

32. d: Expert system

33. b: Palm OS

34. : Application layer

35. c: Thesaurus

36. d: Dialog box

37. c: WiMAX

38. c: High-level architecture

39. : Internet Protocol

40. d: Google

41. : File system

42. a: Blu-ray Disc

43. d: Data structure

44. a: Label

45. a: Turing machine

46. d: Link layer

47. c: Sun Microsystems

48. c: Data integrity

49. a: VistA

50. c: Input device

51. a: Operating system

52. : Shareware

53. d: HTML

54. b: Graphics tablet

55. : System file

56. : SCSI

57. b: System software

58. c: DAVID

59. a: Diagram

Computers

1. a: Windows Firewall

2. a: Propagation delay

3. b: Portable computer

4. c: Packet radio

5. a: Subroutine

6. d: Arithmetic logic unit

7. b: Software

8. c: Local area network

9. a: State diagram

10. d: Mobile phone

11. b: SIMM

12. d: Overclocking

13. c: Hazard

14. : Search engine

15. d: Chain

16. d: Unicode

17. c: Interrupt

18. b: Microarchitecture

19. d: Backplane

20. : Desktop computer

21. b: Desktop publishing

22. : Integrated services

23. b: Harvard architecture

24. : EEPROM

25. d: Wireless

26. a: Malware

27. b: Transport Layer

28. d: Question

29. c: IBM

30. a: Debugging

31. c: Peer-to-peer

32. a: Minicomputer

33. d: Datapath

34. c: Operating system

35. : NAND gate

36. b: Priority encoder

37. c: High-level architecture

38. : Barcode

39. b: DAVID

40. d: Virtual machine

41. b: Vector processor

42. d: Packet switching

43. b: Frequency modulation

44. b: Semiconductor memory

45. b: Data compression

46. a: Interrupt handler

47. a: Internet traffic engineering

48. : Trojan horse

49. d: Optical mesh network

50. c: Device driver

51. : Email

52. c: Secure Digital

53. b: FLOPS

54. d: Memory address

55. d: Expansion card

56. : Cache coherence

57. d: Graphical user interface

58. : Internet

59. d: Multiprocessing

Human-computer interaction

1. d: S-expression

2. d: Website defacement

3. : Design process

4. : Usability

5. b: Surface computer

6. : User interface design

7. b: User interface

8. : Status bar

9. b: Sign language glove

10. a: RWTH FSA Toolkit

11. : Telehaptic

12. b: SDL Passolo

13. a: Spamdexing

14. a: Rumble Pak

15. : Voice Risk Analysis

16. c: Rollover

17. a: EyeToy

18. : Pointing device

19. a: Web accessibility

20. : Debugging

21. c: Rule Interchange Format

22. a: Avatar

23. a: Space

24. d: Speech analytics

25. a: Social information processing

26. a: Web usability

27. a: Information design

28. : Memex

29. c: Smart label

30. d: System Usability Scale

31. c: Query language

32. : Protocol for Web Description Resources

33. c: Virtual globe

34. b: ReCAPTCHA

35. d: Metisse

36. c: Normal mapping

37. c: Planetary scanner

38. b: Virtual engineering

39. : Saddle chair

40. d: Toolbar

41. c: Windows Speech Recognition

42. a: Web life

43. d: Ubiquitous computing

44. c: Virtual fixture

45. a: Virtual Cocoon

46. b: Artificial reality

47. b: Adobe Photoshop

48. a: Space Shuttle Mission 2007

49. d: Virtual world

50. c: Web-based taxonomy

51. c: Virtual keyboard

52. a: TV tuner card

53. d: Hypertext

54. d: Radio button

55. c: Focus group

56. c: Principles of attention stress

57. d: Blog

58. d: Traffic exchange

59. c: SpeechWeb

Software engineering

1. b: Functional programming

2. d: File system

3. : Debugger

4. d: Simula

5. d: Type system

6. : XML schema

7. a: Abstract data type

8. b: Symbol

9. c: Byte

10. b: Sun Microsystems

11. d: ConTeXt

12. c: Software quality

13. a: Prime

14. d: Hash function

15. c: Time-sharing

16. a: Extreme programming

17. b: Preprocessor

18. : SPARC

19. b: Strategy

20. a: High-level architecture

21. : Buffer overflow

22. : Flowchart

23. b: Pseudocode

24. d: Device driver

25. b: Toolbar

26. d: Central processing unit

27. : Binary tree

28. c: SQL injection

29. a: Sequential access

30. d: Semantics

31. a: Unicode

32. d: Identifier

33. d: Simplicity

34. : Html

35. c: Data validation

36. a: Software system

37. b: Object-oriented programming

38. b: MySQL

39. : Usability

40. d: Description

41. c: Bitmap

42. a: Object code

43. : Software engineering

44. a: Sense

45. c: Test case

46. a: Scenario

47. : System testing

48. c: Data dictionary

49. b: Standard library

50. b: Image

51. a: Structure chart

52. c: Hungarian notation

53. a: PowerPC

54. b: Postscript

55. : Tree traversal

56. b: Input device

57. d: Software development

58. b: Metadata

59. d: OpenGL

Computer security

1. : Mobile code

2. c: Simple Mail Transfer Protocol

3. : Wired Equivalent Privacy

4. : Transmission Control Protocol

5. b: Internet

6. a: Security management

7. d: System administrator

8. c: Lattice-based access control

9. a: Cryptography

10. : GetDataBack

11. c: Online Certificate Status Protocol

12. : Single loss expectancy

13. a: Certified Information Systems Auditor

14. c: Computer fraud

15. : Setuid

16. d: Simple Network Management Protocol

17. d: ActiveX

18. b: Netcat

19. c: TACACS

20. c: Replay attack

21. b: Cryptographic hash function

22. b: Log analysis

23. d: SQL injection

24. : Password Safe

25. : Perl

26. a: Web of trust

27. d: Key distribution center

28. b: Timing attack

29. d: Protected Extensible Authentication Protocol

30. b: Multilevel security

31. c: Virtual machine

32. c: Personal firewall

33. b: Access control

34. d: Intrusion prevention system

35. a: IPsec

36. a: Password cracking

37. d: Network Access Control

38. d: Copy protection

39. c: Ciphertext

40. a: Certified Computer Examiner

41. b: Discrete logarithm

42. a: Malware

43. : Ingress filtering

44. a: Tiger team

45. : Risk management

46. d: Reverse engineering

47. : Role-based access control

48. : Security controls

49. b: Secure Hash Standard

50. a: Digital signature

51. a: Linux

52. c: Domain name

53. a: Dynamic Host Configuration Protocol

54. d: Dictionary attack

55. a: Physical layer

56. a: Least privilege

57. b: Search warrant

58. b: Covert channel

59. : SOCKS

Theoretical computer science

1. a: Bandwidth extension

2. a: Computational particle physics

3. c: Reference

4. : Binary moment diagram

5. b: Computer simulation

6. a: Blossom

7. c: Conjugate coding

8. b: Discourse relation

9. d: Expert system

10. : Bi-directional delay line

11. d: Sparse

12. d: Formal verification

13. a: Butcher group

14. : Halton sequence

15. d: Space

16. b: Pushdown automaton

17. a: Code of the Lifemaker

18. d: Bunched logic

19. c: Discrete wavelet transform

20. a: Root-finding algorithm

21. b: BioLinux

22. : Digital physics

23. a: Artificial creation

24. : Deterministic automaton

25. d: Artificial chemistry

26. : Asymptotic equipartition property

27. a: DAVID

28. : Conference on Automated Deduction

29. d: CrossOver

30. b: Discrete system

31. : Compiler

32. : Computational Science

33. a: British Colloquium for Theoretical Computer Science

34. a: Computational Sustainability

35. a: Approximation theory

36. b: Formal language

37. d: Dynamic problem

38. c: Reconstruction filter

39. b: Curse of dimensionality

40. : Coolfluid

41. c: Energy

42. c: Wavelet

43. d: Discrete Laplace operator

44. d: Cylindrification

45. a: Word

46. : Probability distribution

47. : Affine arithmetic

48. b: EPCC

49. d: Evolutionary Acquisition of Neural Topologies

50. c: Activation function

51. a: Gibbs phenomenon

52. a: Weak generative capacity

53. a: MIMO

54. : Delaunay tessellation field estimator

55. d: Automated proof checking

56. d: Abstract family of acceptors

57. b: Fourier analysis

58. b: Iteration

59. a: Laplace transform

Information technology

1. c: Word Lens

2. a: Second Life

3. a: Simplicity

4. : Relational database

5. : Case study

6. b: Space

7. d: Mobile commerce

8. a: Middleware

9. : Google

10. a: Systems design

11. b: Data center

12. b: Best practice

13. b: Business process

14. c: Purchasing

15. b: Online analytical processing

16. d: Access control

17. c: Evaluation

18. b: Symbol

19. d: Virtual reality

20. : IPhone

21. d: Html

22. a: File system

23. : Computer fraud

24. : Artificial intelligence

25. b: Data dictionary

26. : Consumer-to-consumer

27. b: Complexity

28. c: Extranet

29. d: Window

30. a: Word

31. c: Software

32. a: Search engine

33. a: Color

34. : Groupware

35. d: Total cost of ownership

36. d: Column

37. c: System software

38. a: Argument

39. b: Reading

40. a: Information security

41. a: Output device

42. b: Concept

43. : Project management

44. a: Malware

45. d: Code

46. b: Business-to-business

47. b: Read-only memory

48. a: E-commerce

49. d: Operating system

50. : Decision support system

51. b: Visual Basic

52. b: Spreadsheet

53. d: Expert system

54. a: Structure

55. d: Software as a service

56. c: Workflow

57. c: Asset

58. b: Trojan horse

59. : Email

Database management

1. d: B-tree

2. : Network model

3. a: Data dictionary

4. c: Second normal form

5. a: Fact table

6. c: Asset

7. : ODBC

8. d: Fifth normal form

9. d: Foreign key

10. c: Database server

11. b: NewSQL

12. b: Word

13. b: Oracle Database

14. c: Bitmap

15. : Purchasing

16. b: Online analytical processing

17. a: Data validation

18. c: Two-phase locking

19. d: Data quality

20. : Query optimization

21. : Transaction processing

22. d: OLAP cube

23. d: Property

24. b: Serializability

25. a: NoSQL

26. c: Data Definition Language

27. a: Weak entity

28. c: Denormalization

29. c: Middleware

30. b: Database security

31. b: Schedule

32. b: Software

33. b: Search tree

34. : Strategy

35. a: Symbol

36. : Primary key

37. : Structure

38. c: Data Manipulation Language

39. : Hypothetico-deductive model

40. b: Order by

41. a: Transaction log

42. : Database application

43. d: Tablespace

44. a: Functional dependency

45. a: Markup language

46. a: Database model

47. : Snowflake schema

48. d: Relational calculus

49. a: Tuple

50. c: Argument

51. : Teradata

52. a: ROLAP

53. b: Operating system

54. c: Data structure

55. d: Big data

56. : Data store

57. b: Semantics

58. b: ROOT

59. b: METRIC

Artificial intelligence

1. d: Reactive planning

2. a: Epoch

3. : Supervised learning

4. b: Ratio Club

5. a: Martin M. Wattenberg

6. b: Model selection

7. : Lighthill report

8. d: Recursive definition

9. c: Artificial neural network

10. b: Learning Vector Quantization

11. c: Impulse response

12. b: Detailed balance

13. a: AdaBoost

14. : Darwin machine

15. c: ACTION

16. c: Feature extraction

17. : Binary classification

18. a: Euclidean distance

19. d: Automated reasoning

20. d: Recurrent neural network

21. c: Knowledge base

22. b: Distance

23. a: Belief propagation

24. a: Feature vector

25. : Competitive learning

26. b: Optical character recognition

27. c: Conceptual graph

28. : Rational agent

29. b: Mean squared error

30. b: Turing machine

31. a: Autoassociative memory

32. a: Linear classifier

33. : WalkSAT

34. : Lagrange multiplier

35. c: Basis function

36. b: Linear dynamical system

37. b: Commonsense reasoning

38. : Levenshtein distance

39. : Markov model

40. c: Constraint satisfaction

41. : Importance sampling

42. d: Sensitivity analysis

43. a: Linear discriminant analysis

44. : Bayesian inference

45. a: Support vector machine

46. : Empiricism

47. c: Regret

48. d: Synaptic weight

49. b: Situated

50. d: Net Applications

51. b: Lawrence J. Fogel

52. a: Turing test

53. : Logic programming

54. b: Q-learning

55. b: Factor graph

56. d: Computer experiment

57. d: Beam search

58. : Fuzzy clustering

59. d: Latent semantic indexing

Computer networking

1. c: Space

2. c: Authentication

3. a: Structure

4. a: Backbone network

5. a: Cellular network

6. a: Internetworking

7. d: Dynamic Host Configuration Protocol

8. d: Internet layer

9. a: Abstract syntax

10. d: Personal area network

11. d: Ring network

12. c: User Datagram Protocol

13. d: Action

14. : Quadrature amplitude modulation

15. : Directory service

16. : Integrated services

17. : Web server

18. c: Denial-of-service attack

19. c: Trojan horse

20. b: Hypertext Transfer Protocol

21. : Secure Shell

22. d: Peer-to-peer

23. : Routing table

24. c: Building

25. b: Wireless

26. d: Routing Information Protocol

27. : Label switching

28. d: Private network

29. : MAC address

30. d: Access control

31. : Name server

32. : Symbol

33. d: Fault management

34. c: Metro Ethernet

35. c: Broadcast domain

36. b: Multiprotocol Label Switching

37. a: Phoenix Technologies

38. : Virtual circuit

39. d: Private IP

40. a: Internet Society

41. d: Network management

42. b: Domain name

43. : Network address translation

44. a: Token ring

45. : Traffic shaping

46. b: End system

47. a: Internet traffic engineering

48. d: Transmission Control Protocol

49. b: Fibre Channel

50. a: Virtual LAN

51. : Cryptography

52. c: Patch panel

53. c: Task manager

54. : Simple Mail Transfer Protocol

55. a: Propagation delay

56. : Command Prompt

57. b: File server

58. a: Quality of service

59. : Optical fiber

CPSIA information can be obtained
at www.ICGtesting.com
Printed in the USA
FSHW022018290721
83692FS

9 781538 846902